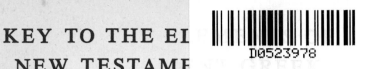

KEY TO THE EL
NEW TESTAME

J. W. WENHAM

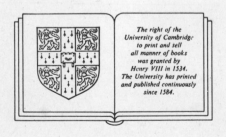

The right of the
University of Cambridge
to print and sell
all manner of books
was granted by
Henry VIII in 1534.
The University has printed
and published continuously
since 1584.

CAMBRIDGE UNIVERSITY PRESS

CAMBRIDGE

NEW YORK   PORT CHESTER

MELBOURNE   SYDNEY

ON THE USE OF A KEY

A Key can be more hindrance than help in learning a language, if it is not used in a disciplined way. It is quite wrong to consult the Key at each difficulty and at each lapse of memory. Ideally, *a whole exercise should be completed and carefully revised before reference is made to the Key.* Failing this, several sentences should be done at a time before they are corrected.

3A

In Exercises 3 to 6 the Greek Present is translated by the Present Continuous to emphasise the idea of continuity, which is the primary idea of the Greek tense. Often the Present Simple will give a better rendering, since the Present Continuous can be a clumsy over-translation. But it is good at this stage to emphasise the fundamental idea. After Exercise 6 the Present Simple may be used, providing it gives good sense in the context.

He (she or it) is loosing. (*With such words the translation 'he' will in future be given, though 'she' or 'it' is always possible.*) We are loosing, they are loosing, you (pl.) are loosing, you (sing.) are loosing. We are finding, he is writing, you (pl.) are throwing; you (sing.) are seeing, they are raising. Do they say? You (pl.) are judging, we are throwing, I am eating, they are sending, you (pl.) arc taking, wc arc saving, hc is remaining. Do you (sing.) have? Do I know? You (pl.) are healing.

3B

Λυομεν, λυουσιν, λυεις, λυετε, λυει, λυουσιν, λυει. ἐχετε; σωζει· θεραπευουσιν; βαλλω· ἐγειρει, κρινομεν, μενεις, κρινετε· πεμπει; γραφετε, ἐσθιεις, εὑρισκει, λαμβανομεν, βλεπουσιν. λεγεις;

4A

We are speaking, you (sing.) are asking, they are keeping, you (pl.) are doing. Is he repenting? They are bearing witness, you (pl.) are seeking. I am calling; we are looking at, you (sing.) are keeping, I am hating. Is he blaspheming? (*or*, Does he blaspheme?) They are blessing, we are loving, you (pl.) are throwing, I know (*English does not use the Present Continuous in this case, cf. 5A7, 10*), you (sing.) are raising. Have they? (*or*, Do they have?) He is healing, you (pl.) are judging, we are remaining, they are saving.

4B

Ζητουσιν, αἰτει, καλεις, μαρτυρουμεν, λαλω · τηρειτε, ποιει. θεωρειτε; φιλουμεν, καλουσιν, αἰτει, ποιουσιν, ζητουμεν, μαρτυρουσιν, θεωρει. βλασφημουσιν; μετανοει. μισουμεν· εὑλογειτε. καλω. γραφομεν, ἐσθιουσιν, εὑρισκει, κρινει, πεμπεις.

5A

1. O Israel, are you (pl.) seeking death? 2. An angel is saving a people. 3. A lord is writing words. 4. You (pl.) are keeping laws. 5. Do Pharisees love Christ? 6. You (pl.) are looking at fields. 7. He has a throne. 8. He is hating a world and seeking a friend. 9. Leper, are you blaspheming? 10. We know death. 11. I am throwing stones. 12. Servants (deacons) are bearing witness. 13. We are blessing teachers. 14. Is an apostle healing a paralysed man? 15. Jews and Pharisees are asking for friends. 16. He is healing eyes. 17. Fear is taking brethren and people. 18. Are you (sing.) seeking for an elder? 19. We are making a river. 20. I have enemies.

5B

1. Ἀγγελος καλει ἀνθρωπον. 2. ἀδελφος ἐχει ἀγρον. 3. κυριοι πεμπουσιν ἀγγελους. 4. λογους γραφουσιν. 5. εὑρισκετε λιθον; 6. Χριστος κρινει ἀνθρωπους και ἀγγελους. 7. τηρεις νομους; 8. ἀνθρωπος και ἀγγελος ζητουσιν τοπον. 9. μαρτυρουμεν και λαος μετανοει. 10. Κυριε, μενεις. 11. ἀποστολοι λαλουσιν και διακονοι ἐχουσιν φοβον. 12. ποιεις θρονον; 13. μισουσιν Χριστον και φιλουσιν θανατον. 14. πρεσβυτερος λαλει. 15. σωζει λεπρους και παραλυτικους και θεραπευει ὀφθαλμους. 16. Φαρισαιοι γραφουσιν νομους; 17. Ἰουδαιοι, γινωσκομεν Χριστον. 18. λογους κρινει; 19. θεωρω ποταμον. 20. λυει φιλον. 21. ζητειτε κοσμον. 22. Ἰσραηλ λεγει, Χριστος σωζει;

6A

1. He is writing the law of the Lord. 2. The men are seeking the angels. 3. The slaves are making a way for the Lord. 4. The brother of the slave is seeing the house. 5. They are keeping the word of God. 6. Jesus is blessing the bread and the wine of the enemy. 7. The devil hates the temple (shrine) of God. 8. Are you (pl.) eating the fruit? 9. The Lord is saving sinners. 10. The Jews are making a cross for Jesus. 11. Virgins know the words of

4

the crowd.　12. The sun and the wind are healing.　13. The law is for the world.　14. The wine is the (a) reward.

6B

1. Χρονος (καιρος) μενει;　2. ζητειτε τους οὐρανους;　3. Ἰακω-βος ἐχει μισθον τῳ υἱῳ.　4. βλεπομεν ἐρημον.　5. ὁ ἀγγελος γραφει νομους τῳ κοσμῳ.　6. ὁ του ἀνθρωπου δουλος ποιει ἀρτον. 7. ὁ διαβολος ζητει καιρον τοις του Χριστου πειρασμοις.　8. ἁμαρ-τωλοι βλεπουσιν τους λογους των ἀποστολων και μετανοουσιν. 9. ὁ Ἰησους λεγει τῳ ὀχλῳ, Φιλειτε τον Θεον;　10. οἱ ἀποστολοι γινωσκουσιν τον Κυριον.　11. ὁ Υἱος του Θεου ζητει τους οὐρανους;　12. μισουσιν πειρασμον.　13. ἐχεις οἰκον και ἀγρους, ἀρτον και οἰνον;　14. εὑρισκομεν τον τοπον ναῳ.　15. ἀνθρωπος και διακονος λαμβανουσιν τον καρπον του πρεσβυτερου.　16. ὁ Θεος μισθος ἐστιν και ὁ μισθος Θεος ἐστιν.

7A

1. The Pharisees of the council hate Jesus.　2. The demons know (the) Christ and have fear.　3. The apostles speak the gospel to lords and slaves.　4. We are keeping the Sabbath (or, Sabbaths). 5. The teachers speak the mysteries of heaven to the children.　6. The men have sheep and a boat.　7. Are you looking at the face of Jesus? 8. The slaves take the trees for James.　9. The brother is seeking the tomb of the child.　10. You are doing the works of the Devil. 11. The Jews are writing books.　12. We are seeing the signs of the times.　13. He is finding silver.　14. The servants are keeping the cups of the temple of Jerusalem.　15. Is a virgin making a garment for Jesus?　16. The mystery is the gospel.

From now on the choice of a singular or plural translation for the second person singular is arbitrary. In most cases either is correct.

In Lesson 6 we noted that abstract nouns 'often' have the article. It is equally true that they often do *not* have the article. The usage cannot be reduced to simple rules. The answers given in this key attempt to follow the predominant New Testament practice, but in many cases either the inclusion or the omission of the article is possible.

7 B

1. Χριστος εὐλογει το ποτηριον οἰνου και τον ἀρτον.   2. γινωσκεις τα σημεια του Υἱου του ἀνθρωπου;   3. ὁ Κυριος σωζει (τους) ἀνθρωπους και (τα) τεκνα.   4. τα τεκνα αἰτει τους πρεσβυτερους ἱματια.   5. βλεπετε τα προβατα;   6. μαρτυρουμεν τῳ εὐαγγελιῳ του Θεου. 7. οἱ Ἰουδαιοι φιλουσιν το σαββατον και (τα) Ἱεροσολυμα (or (την) Ἱερουσαλημ).   8. ἀγγελοι θεωρουσιν το προσωπον του Θεου. 9. τα δαιμονια φιλει τα μνημεια;   10. το συνεδριον κρινει ἁμαρτωλους. 11. παιδια γινωσκει τα μυστηρια των οὐρανων.   12. ὁ Ἰησους πεμπει το πλοιον.   13. φιλουμεν τα του ἱερου βιβλια.   14. βλεπομεν τοπον δενδρων.   15. ὁ Θεος μισει τα ἐργα του διαβολου και ἁμαρτωλων.   16. οἱ ἀποστολοι ἐχουσιν ἀργυριον;   17. το σαββατον σημειον του Θεου ἐστιν.

8 A

1. The brothers know the love of God.   2. The beginning of the gospel of Jesus Christ, Son of God.   3. The apostles are writing the letters.   4. The Pharisees of the synagogue are seeking righteousness. 5. We are blessing the steadfastness of (the) Christ.   6. The scriptures bear witness to (the) Christ.   7. Are you keeping the commandments?   8. The teachers are looking at the cloud.   9. Jesus speaks the parables to the people of the village.   10. We know the sound of the crowd.   11. We love the house of prayer.   12. The anger of God remains.   13. The slaves ask for peace.   14. Christ is the bread of life.   15. Are you saving the soul?   16. We are eating the fruit of the earth.   17. Do the apostles have the honour of men?   18. The angel finds the prison (guard).

8 B

1. Ὁ Θεος κρινει την γην.   2. γινωσκετε τας ἐντολας.   3. οἱ ἀποστολοι φιλουσιν την του Θεου διαθηκην.   4. ἐχει ἀργυριον, την τιμην ἀγρου.   5. οἱ πρεσβυτεροι της κωμης βαλλουσιν λιθους.

6. ὁ Θεος σωζει τας ψυχας των ἀνθρωπων. 7. ὁ Ἰακωβος πεμπει ἐπιστολην τῳ φιλῳ του ἀποστολου. 8. βλεπω το ποτηριον της ὀργης του Θεου. 9. ὁ Θεος ἀγαπη και δικαιοσυνη ἐστιν. 10. πεμπεις τους λογους του εὐαγγελιου της εἰρηνης. 11. οἱ δουλοι μισουσιν την φυλακην. 12. τα τεκνα λαμβανει τα βιβλια της γραφης; 13. ὁ Θεος γινωσκει τας προσευχας των ἀνθρωπων. 14. ὁ μισθος της ὑπομονης ζωη ἐστιν. 15. Ἰσραηλ γινωσκει την διδαχην των ἐντολων.

9A

1. The kingdom of heaven is life and truth. 2. God hates un-righteousness and sin. 3. Does the generation of sinners repent? 4. Christ is the head of the Church. 5. Do demons have authority? 6. We are seeing the beginning of the day. 7. God sends the word of promise. 8. The Pharisees keep the commandments of (the) sacrifice. 9. The fruit of God is love, joy and peace. 10. Men see the face and God sees the heart. 11. (The) sinners have a place of repentance. 12. Have the widows bread for the children? 13. Peter blesses the Lord of the earth and sea. 14. The tongues of the apostles speak words of the wisdom of God. 15. The hour of Christ's glory is joy for the angels. 16. We are making a house of stones. 17. The witness of love is making a way for the coming of the Lord. 18. Galilee and Judaea know the needs of the widows.

9B

1. Ζητουσιν τον καιρον της ἐπαγγελιας. 2. οἱ ἀγγελοι των οὐρανων ἐχουσιν την χαραν. 3. ὁ Παυλος μαρτυρει τῃ ἀληθειᾳ του εὐαγγελιου και τῃ σοφιᾳ του Θεου. 4. ἡ μετανοια θυρα της σωτηριας ἐστιν. 5. τα παιδια μετανοει; 6. ἡ θυρα του μνημειου ἐστιν λιθος. 7. ὁ Θεος ποιει τας θαλασσας, τας πετρας της γης και τας νεφελας των οὐρανων. 8. ἡ χρεια της χηρας χαρα ἐστιν. 9. Χριστος ἐχει την ἐξουσιαν του Θεου. 10. ἡ ἐκκλησια βασιλεια ἐστιν του Θεου; 11. ὁ Θεος μισει την των ἀνθρωπων ἀδικιαν. 12. ὁ Ἰησους θεραπευει τον υἱον της χηρας. 13. ἡ γενεα του διαβολου βλασφημει. 14. γινωσκετε την ὡραν

πειρασμου; 15. Παυλος ἐσθιει τας θυσιας; 16. ζητει καρδιαν της εἰρηνης και της δικαιοσυνης. 17. ἡ χαρα Παυλου σταυρος Χριστου ἐστιν. 18. ζητουσιν την ἡμεραν (της) σωτηριας. 19. αἱ γλωσσαι των ἀποστολων λαλουσιν λογους της ἀληθειας τῳ λαῳ.

Revision Test 1

The only question which cannot be immediately checked from the text-book is No. 5: 1. Τῃ θαλασσῃ. 2. της ἐρημου. 3. της ἀγαπης. 4. τῳ ποτηριῳ. 5. της γλωσσης. 6. της ὁδου. 7. τῳ Ἰησου.

10A

1. Hypocrite, you are keeping the commandments, but you do not love God.   2. The disciples therefore are remaining in the house.   3. Jesus says (tells) the parable to the disciples and the tax-collector.   4. Christ then is the judge of men in the day of wrath.   5. Are the workmen throwing stones into the sea?   6. Elijah the prophet calls the people.   7. In the day of glory we see Christ face to face.   8. He is Jesus; for he is saving the people from sin.   9. But the angel is loosing Peter from (the) prison.   10. Judas does not love Jesus or (nor) the disciples.   11. John knows the brother of Judah.   12. And Jesus raises the young man from death.   13. Therefore we hate the works of Satan.   14. The soldiers keep the words of John the Baptist and repent, but the Pharisees do not repent, for they do not have the love of God.

10B

Note: 'towards' will be translated προς, 'into' εἰς, 'away from' ἀπο, out of' ἐκ. But the choice of προς or εἰς when translating 'to', and ἀπο or ἐκ when translating 'from', is often arbitrary.

1. Λεγει οὖν ὁ Ἰησους, Ὁ Υἱος του ἀνθρωπου ἐστιν ἐν ταις των οὐρανων νεφελαις.   2. οἱ Ἰουδαιοι ζητουσιν την φωνην του προφητου ἐν τῃ ἐρημῳ.   3. οἱ υἱοι του Θεου τηρουσιν τας ἐντολας ἐκ καρδιας;   4. οἱ τελωναι βλασφημουσιν;   5. οἱ ἀρα μαθηται ἐχουσιν την ἀγαπην του Θεου.   6. οἱ ἐργαται οὐχ

εὑρισκουσιν τὴν ὁδον εἰς τον σταυρον, και τὴν θυσιαν του Ἰησου οὐ
θεωρουσιν.   7. οἱ δε ὑποκριται οὐ γινωσκουσιν τὴν ζωην ἀλλα
μενουσιν ἐν (τῃ) ἁμαρτιᾳ.   8. Χριστος λαλει ἐν παραβολαις τοις
νεανιαις· ζητουσιν γαρ τὴν ἀληθειαν.   9. ἀπο της ἀρχης του
κοσμου ὁ Χριστος Κυριος ἐστιν.   10. ὁ κριτης οὐ λαμβανει το
ἀργυριον ἀπο των πρεσβυτερων της ἐκκλησιας, οὐδε μισει τους
ἀποστολους.   11. οἱ στρατιωται βαλλουσιν Ἀνδρεαν τον ἀποστολον
εἰς φυλακην.   12. βλεπετε τοις ὀφθαλμοις της ἀγαπης.   13. Ἰωανης ὁ Βαπτιστης καλει τον λαον εἰς μετανοιαν.   14. οἱ Φαρισαιοι
ζητουσιν σημεια ἐξ οὐρανου.   15. Ἠλειας οὐ φιλει τας θυσιας
(των) ἁμαρτωλων, τα ἐργα Σατανα.

11 A

1. The unbelieving Jews are not repenting.   2. In the last days few
have love.   3. The beloved apostle is first writing a new letter to the
church.   4. Jesus heals the blind and the lepers.   5. Are the
disciples eating the unclean fruit?   6. God is judging each young
man.   7. The paralysed man is in the midst of the temple and is
blessing the beautiful works of God.   8. The poor love the gospel.

11 B

1. Σοφαι παρθενοι.   2. (ἡ) ἱκανη ὑπομονη· (ἡ) ὑπομονη (ἡ)
ἱκανη.   3. ἡ καινη ζωη· ἡ ζωη ἡ καινη.   4. καλοι θρονοι.
5. πιστα παιδια.   6. ἀπιστοι προσευχαι.   7. κακους καιρους.
8. ἐν τῃ τριτῃ ἡμερᾳ· ἐν τῃ ἡμερᾳ τῃ τριτῃ.   9. το ἱματιον του
πτωχου. (του πτωχου ἀνθρωπου and του ἀνθρωπου του πτωχου are
possible, but not so idiomatic.)   10. ἡ πρωτη προσευχη· ἡ προσευχη
ἡ πρωτη.   11. ὁ μονος Θεος· ὁ Θεος ὁ μονος.   12. αἱ ἁμαρτιαι
των ἀπιστων.   13. καινα βιβλια.   14. ἀκαθαρτον προβατον και
ἀκαθαρτος ψυχη.   15. ἀγαθη καρδια.   16. ἡ ἐσχατη ὡρα· ἡ
ὡρα ἡ ἐσχατη.   17. αἰωνιοι γραφαι.   18. ἀγαπητη χηρα.
19. ὀλιγα πλοια των μαθητων.   20. δυνατοι ἀγγελοι.   21. ἐν
μεσῳ του ποταμου.   22. τυφλε ὑποκριτα.

11 C

(In the following sentences only one of the two possible attributive renderings will be given.)

1. Οἱ λοιποι εὑρισκουσιν τον μονον νεανιαν ἐν τῃ ἐρημῳ.   2. οἱ κακοι προφηται οὐ μαρτυρουσιν τῃ ἀληθειᾳ.   3. οἱ στρατιωται πρωτον ποιουσιν καινον σταυρον τῳ Υἱῳ του Θεου.   4. ἀγαθοι λογοι σωζουσιν (τους) ἀνθρωπους ἐκ του θανατου.   5. μονος Παυλος μενει πιστος;   6. ὁ Ἀνδρεας πρωτος μαθητης του Χριστου ἐστιν.   7. οἱ σοφοι οὐ γινωσκουσιν τον Θεον τῃ σοφιᾳ, ἀλλ' οἱ πτωχοι ζητουσιν την βασιλειαν του Θεου.   8. ὁ Ἰησους, ἀνθρωπος δυνατος ἐν λογοις και ἐργοις.   9. ὁ διακονος ἐστιν ἀγαθος στρατιωτης Ἰησου Χριστῳ.   10. τα λοιπα παιδια αἰτει ἀρτον ἀπο των ἀδελφων του Ἰησου.   11. οἱ φιλοι ἐχουσιν ἱκανον ἀργυριον.   12. Παυλος θεωρει τον τριτον οὐρανον.   13. ὁ ἐσχατος ἐχθρος θανατος ἐστιν.

12 A

1. God is raising Jesus from the dead.   2. Blessed are the pure in heart.   3. The Son of Man does not seek his own glory but the glory of God.   4. Does the rich man love the poor?   5. The righteous are sons of God.   6. The saints see the glory of the heavens and bear witness to the voices of the angels.   7. Christ has a third temptation in the desert.

12 B

1. Ἡ νεφελη μικρα· μικρα ἡ νεφελη.   2. ὁ πονηρος ὀφθαλμος· ὁ ὀφθαλμος ὁ πονηρος.   3. οἱ νομοι παλαιοι· παλαιοι οἱ νομοι. 4. ἡ ἁγια ζωη· ἡ ζωη ἡ ἁγια.   5. ἡ δευτερα ὡρα· ἡ ὡρα ἡ δευτερα. 6. οἱ υἱοι ἐλευθεροι· ἐλευθεροι οἱ υἱοι.   7. οἱ καινοι οὐρανοι (οἱ οὐρανοι οἱ καινοι) και ἡ καινη γη (ἡ γη ἡ καινη).   8. τα δαιμονια ἰσχυρα; ἰσχυρα τα δαιμονια;   9. ὁ ἰδιος μισθος· ὁ μισθος ὁ ἰδιος. 10. ἡ δικαια ψυχη· ἡ ψυχη ἡ δικαια.   11. ἡ γενεα πλουσια· πλουσια ἡ γενεα.   12. ὁ δεξιος ὀφθαλμος· ὁ ὀφθαλμος ὁ δεξιος. 13. ἡ ἀγαπη καθαρα; καθαρα ἡ ἀγαπη;

12 C

1. Ὁ διακονος του Ἠλειου βλεπει μικραν νεφελην ἐν τοις οὐρανοις.
2. εἶ ἀξιος; 3. οἱ ἐχθροι Χριστου εἰσιν τεκνα του διαβολου.
4. εἶ ὁ Χριστος. 5. οἱ πονηροι βλεπουσιν τον δευτερον θανατον,
οὐ γαρ φιλουσιν την σοφιαν του Θεου. 6. ὀλιγοι εὑρισκουσιν την
ὁδον της ζωης. 7. ὁ παλαιος οἰνος ἐστιν ἀγαθος, ὁ δε νεος ἐστιν
κακος. 8. ὁ ἰσχυρος λυει τον δουλον ἐκ της φυλακης. 9. ἐσμεν
ὁμοιοι προβατοις. 10. ἐστιν ἑτερον μνημειον; 11. οἱ πλουσιοι
οὐκ εἰσιν ἐλευθεροι ἀπο (ἐκ) της ἐξουσιας του Θεου. 12. εἰμι ὁ
πρωτος και ὁ ἐσχατος. 13. ὠ ὑποκριτα, εἶ ὁ δουλος νεκρων ἐργων.
14. οἱ τελωναι ἐχουσιν καρπους ἀξιους της μετανοιας τω Ἰησου.
15. ἡ προσευχη του Φαρισαιου οὐκ ἐστιν καθαρα. 16. ἐχει
ἑτεραν ἐξουσιαν. 17. ἡ διδαχη ἡ παλαια οὐκ ἐστιν ὁμοια ταις
παραβολαις του Κυριου. 18. ἐστε ἐχθροι του σταυρου του Χριστου.
19. μακαριαι εἰσιν αἱ των μαθητων καρδιαι.

13 A

1. Jesus used to receive small children, and the small children used to
hear Jesus. 2. The sinners were not obeying the prophet.
3. Paul was teaching the gospel and you were believing the words.
4. He was reading in the book of the old law. 5. But Christ carries a
cross and abounds in love. 6. The holy angel was opening a door in
heaven. 7. The rich young man therefore was departing to his own
house. 8. We are rejoicing in the Lord, for he is leading the church
into (the) truth. 9. Was Christ sending (throwing) (or, Used Christ
to send) the evil men out of the temple? 10. The righteous were not
offering sacrifices in a different temple. 11. We were weeping and
prophesying wrath from heaven. 12. For the council was recognising
the wisdom of the widow's teaching. 13. But the workman puts a
garment on the child and persuades the elders by a parable. 14. We
used to bring the money to the tax-collector, but he used to persecute
(the) rich and (the) poor. 15. The enemies of the people were dying
in prison, but the judge was releasing a few slaves. 16. He used
not to teach the children, nor lead his own generation away from the
ways of unrighteousness.

13B

1. Ἐδιδασκον το εὐαγγελιον τοις μαθηταις.   2. αἱ παρθενοι
ὑπηγον ἐκ του οἰκου.   3. ἐφερον το του δουλου πλοιον εἰς την
θαλασσαν.   4. οἱ προφηται ἐδιδασκον τα τεκνα ἐν τοις οἰκοις.
5. προσεφερετε την τιμην τῳ Κυριῳ, (ὠ) ἀγγελοι.   6. ὑποκριτα,
ὑπηκουες τῳ ὀχλῳ.   7. συνηγον τα προβατα προς τα δενδρα.
8. το παιδιον ἀνεγινωσκεν τας γραφας ἐν τῳ ἱερῳ.   9. ἀπηγομεν
τους στρατιωτας ἀπο της θαλασσης.   10. Ἰωανης ὁ βαπτιστης
οὐκ ἐποιει σημεια.   11. ὁ Κυριος ἠγεν τους μαθητας εἰς την ἐρημον.
12. ἐπειθετε οὐν τον λαον.   13. οἱ ἁγιοι ἐχαιρον, ἀλλ' ἡ ἁμαρτια
ἐπερισσευεν.   14. ἐξεβαλλεν δαιμονια;   15. παρελαμβανομεν την
κεφαλην του Ἰακωβου.   16. ἀπελυετε τους δουλους.   17. ἐ-
κλαιον και ἀπεθνησκον, οὐ γαρ ἠκουον του Κυριου οὐδε την
ἐπαγγελιαν.   18. ὁ Ἰησους ἠνοιγεν τους ὀφθαλμους των τυφλων,
και ἐπεγινωσκον τους ἰδιους φιλους.   19. ἐδιωκεν την ἀπιστον
χηραν.

14A

1. These men were dying in the desert.   2. But I was (they were)
throwing those trees into the sea.   3. These women were remaining
in the boat.   4. For God is saving these women from the evil one.
5. For we do not judge these things.   6. Were we saying these
promises in the church?   7. But those men were throwing out
demons.   8. In that day they were blessing the wisdom of the Lord.
9. In that hour we were rejoicing.   10. But he used to take the wine
and give thanks to God.   11. We were exhorting and calling, but
they were not following.   12. But the whole crowd was doing wrong
and was not serving nor worshipping God.   13. The children were
ill, but the rich man walked in the ways of unrighteousness.   14. The
evil soldier holds and binds the workman to the tree.   15. The poor
were marrying and dwelling in the land.   16. The wise lord therefore
has mercy on the righteous and builds houses for the widows.
17. For the whole synagogue seemed like sheep.

14B

1. Αὕτη ἠκολουθει τῳ νεανιᾳ. 2. ἐκεινος ὁ πονηρος διακονος ἐδει τον ἰδιον υἱον. 3. οὑτοι οἱ πρεσβυτεροι δοκουσιν τυφλοι. ('Seem' is a verb of incomplete predication (E.G. 7 B), so both subject and complement are nominative.) 4. ὁ μακαριος πρεσβυτερος ἐφωνει ὁλον τον ὀχλον. 5. οὑτος οὐν ὁ δευτερος ἀδελφος διηκονει και προσεκυνει τῳ Θεῳ ἐν ἑτερῳ ἱερῳ. 6. οἱ παραλυτικοι περιεπατουν, οἱ πλουσιοι παρεκαλουν τους πτωχους, οἱ ἰσχυροι ᾠκοδομουν οἰκιας τοις πρεσβυτεροις, ὁλος ὁ λαος ηὐχαριστει. 7. γαμουσιν και κατοικουσιν ἐν τῃ κωμῃ ἐν εἰρηνῃ και τιμῃ. 8. ἠλεει τους ἁγιους, ἠσθενουν γαρ. 9. ὁ διαβολος κρατει μικρα παιδια και ἀδικει την ἐκκλησιαν. 10. ὁ γαρ Κυριος σωζει τας ψυχας των ἀνθρωπων ἀπο του πονηρου. 11. ἡ ἀγαπη και ἡ ἀληθεια εἰσιν ἐν τῃ αἰωνιῳ βασιλειᾳ του Θεου. 12. ἐν δε ἐκεινῃ τῃ ἡμερᾳ ἠκουομεν το εὐαγγελιον και ἐξεβαλλομεν δαιμονια.

15A

1. We were looking at their houses. 2. This man was a disciple of John the Baptist. 3. For we were slaves of sin. 4. You were therefore servants of the people. 5. His sons were bad. 6. For this was his commandment. 7. The rest of the women of the village were gathering their sheep together in the middle of the field. 8. Jesus himself was not worshipping, but his disciples. 9. Life remains in them. 10. Those were different loaves and another cup. 11. You were a hypocrite and we were blind. 12. I was beloved, but you were hating one another. 13. You were an evil woman.

15B

1. Τουτο το προσωπον· το προσωπον τουτο. 2. ὁλον το προσωπον· το προσωπον ὁλον. 3. αὐτο το προσωπον· το προσωπον αὐτο. 4. ἐκεινο το προσωπον· το προσωπον ἐκεινο. 5. το αὐτο προσωπον· το προσωπον το αὐτο. 6. το ἀλλο προσωπον· το προσωπον το ἀλλο. 7. το ἰδιον προσωπον· το προσωπον το ἰδιον.

8. ἕτερον πρόσωπον.   9. τα πρόσωπα ἀλλήλων.   10. ἔπειθον
ἑαυτους.

15 C

1. Ἐν ἀρχῇ ἦν ὁ Λόγος.   2. αὕτη ἐστιν ἡ ἀγάπη του Θεου.   3. οἱ
αὐτοι μαθηται ηὐχαριστουν τῳ πλουσιῳ τελωνῃ.   4. ἐβλέπετε τους
υἱους αὐτης ἐν τῳ οἰκῳ.   5. αὐτοι παρελαμβανομεν αὐτους εἰς το
ἕτερον πλοιον.   6. ἦτε ἐν τῳ ἱερῳ ἐν ἐκειναις ταις ἡμεραις.
7. αὕτη ἐστιν ἡ αἰωνιος ζωη.   8. ἦσαν ἁγιοι και ἀγαπητοι.
9. τα τεκνα αὐτων ἦν ἐν τῃ ἐκκλησιᾳ.   10. ἀνεγινωσκον τας
γραφας ἀλλήλοις ἐν τῃ συναγωγῃ.   11. οἱ αὐτοι Ἰουδαιοι
οὗτοι ἠκουον και ἠκολουθουν τοις ἰδιοις προφηταις.   12. ὁ
βαπτιστης αὐτος ἐδιδασκεν τους μαθητας αὐτου.   13. ἀλλο παιδιον
βαλλει ἑαυτο εἰς την θαλασσαν.

16 A

1. We speak according to (the) truth.   2. I (they) used to go with the
soldiers by day.   3. The teacher is above the disciple.   4. The
same widow was walking round the village.   5. I was teaching daily
in the temple.   6. The Lord was speaking through his prophet (or,
possibly, the prophet himself).   7. You are not under law, but under
love.   8. He was dying upon the throne of Israel.   9. He was an
angel from God.   10. They walk with one another beside the sea.
11. We were sinners before God.   12. Before the shrine is the
judge's throne.   13. Before that hour they were not seeing his glory
nor hearing his voice.   14. The tax-collectors with other sinners
were finding salvation.   15. It was about the third hour.
16. Through man is death, but Christ keeps his own disciples until
his coming.   17. Apart from him we are weak.

16 B

1. Ὑπηγον κατ' ἰδιαν εἰς τας ἰδιας οἰκιας.   2. ὁ Θεος ἠγεν
αὐτους δια (του) πειρασμου ἀχρι (ἑως) της ἐσχατης ἡμερας.   3. ὁ
Θεος ἐστιν ὑπερ του λαου αὐτου, ἀλλ' οἱ ἐργαται Σατανα εἰσιν κατα

της ἐκκλησιας.   4. ὁ πονηρος ἐστιν νεκρος δι᾽ ἁμαρτιαν (δια την
ἁμαρτιαν).   5. μετα τουτο ἐλαλουμεν ἀλληλοις.   6. γινωσκουσιν
περι ἱματια (ἱματιων) χωρις της διδαχης του βιβλιου.   7. εἰμι γαρ
ἀνθρωπος ὑπο ἐξουσιαν.   8. μενει παρ᾽ αὐτῳ ταυτην την ἡμεραν.
9. βαλλει λιθους ἐπι τους ἀγρους του ἐχθρου αὐτου.   10. πτωχοι
ἠσαν ἐν τῳ Ἰσραηλ ἐπι Ἡλειου του προφητου.   11. (ἐν) τῃ τριτῃ
ἡμερᾳ ἐζητουν σημειον παρ᾽ αὐτου ἐκ του οὐρανου.   12. ἡ της
σωτηριας χαρα περισσευει χωρις του νομου.

17A

1. You were being sent by the teachers to a different crowd.   2. In
this place we were beholding with the (our) eyes the Lord of
heaven. (Greek often does not use a possessive pronoun with parts of
the body.)   3. These words were being spoken by the apostles
before the elders.   4. And the sheep were being pursued with stones
by the children.   5. We were being sent with the prophets before
the crowd.   6. Because of this you were being persuaded by the
words of the judges.   7. Before these things the tax-collectors were
being taught with the young men.   8. The sons themselves were
eating the same loaves.   9. O blind hypocrite, you do not walk
according to the ways of the law.   10. A cross was being made by
the workmen for each saint in Jerusalem.   11. The friends were
sending a few loaves to one another, and a little wine and sufficient
money to the worthy brothers in prison.   12. O Jerusalem, you are
not being found faithful, for you are against the truth.   13. We were
being encouraged by the words of the covenant at that time.   14. We
were leading the clean sacrifices through the temple after the rich men
of the council.   15. After those days the remaining (rest of the)
soldiers departed out of the village.   16. You used to weep for the
faithless and the unclean.

17B

1. Ὁ λογος του Θεου ἀνεγινωσκετο ὑπο των ἀποστολων.   2. το
μνημειον ᾠκοδομειτο ὑπο το ἱερον.   3. δια τουτο οἱ κριται
ἐπειθοντο ὑπο των πιστων διδασκαλων.   4. ἠγες τον λαον ὀπισω

τοῦ ἀγαπητοῦ προφητοῦ διὰ τῆς ἐρήμου εἰς τὰ Ἱεροσόλυμα.   5. μετὰ
τοῦτο ἐζητοῦντο ὑπὸ ὅλου τοῦ ὄχλου.   6. οἱ λίθοι ἦσαν ἐπὶ τῇ
γῇ ὑπὲρ τὸν ποταμον.   7. ὁ θρόνος ἐφέρετο ὑπὸ τῶν ἐργατῶν εἰς
ἄλλον τόπον παρὰ τὸν οἶκον.   8. ὁ κόσμος ἐποιεῖτο διὰ τοῦ
Υἱοῦ τοῦ Θεου.   9. ὦ ὑποκριτά, οὐ λαλεῖς περὶ τῶν ἐντολῶν τοῦ
Κυρίου.   10. αὐτοὶ οἱ νεανίαι ἐδιδάσκοντο ὑπὸ τῶν ἰδίων
διδασκαλων.   11. μετ᾽ οὖν ταῦτα ἐλαλοῦμεν τὸν λόγον τοῦ Θεου
τοῖς μαθηταῖς.   12. ἠγείρεσθε τοῖς δυνατοῖς λόγοις τῆς ὀργῆς
τοῦ προφητου.

18A

1. Take the cup and rejoice in this second sign of righteousness, peace
and life.   2. It is the beginning of authority which seems like new
wine.   3. Therefore seek the face of the Lord in prayer on the
Sabbath.   4. In time of temptation offer the sacrifice of repentance
and do works of steadfastness.   5. Let them be seen by the wise.
6. Be raised from the dead.   7. Be healed by prayer.   8. Lord,
heal the right eye of the free servant.   9. Was not the first woman
last?   10. The dead are not happy, are they?   11. He was not
calling bad men to the fear of God, was he?   *Or,* Could he have been
calling bad men to the fear of God?   12. Let the Holy One be
blessed.   13. Be persuaded by the elders; do not obey the young
men.   14. Open each door, for this is possible with God.   15. Put
righteousness on the heart and let sacrifices be offered in the midst of
the sanctuary.   16. Do not let him be judged nor injured.

Note: The verbs in 3, 4, 7, 14 could be Indicative.

18B

1. Διὸ βαλλέσθω παρὰ τὴν ὁδόν.   2. λύου ἀπὸ (ἐκ) τῆς ἁμαρτίας
καθ᾽ ἡμέραν.   3. σῴζεσθε ἀπὸ (ἐκ) τῆς ἐξουσίας πονηρῶν.   4. αὗ-
ται αἱ ἐντολαὶ τηρείσθωσαν.   5. ἀπαγέσθω εἰς τὸ συνέδριον τοῦ
Σατανᾶ.   6. οἱ καθαροὶ μὴ κατοικείτωσαν ἐν μέσῳ τῆς ἁμαρτίας,
μηδὲ ἀκάθαρτοι καρδίαι ἐχέτωσαν (τὴν) χαρὰν ἐν τοῖς μισθοῖς τῶν
πλουσίων.   7. ἦν καλὸν πλοῖον ἐπὶ τῇ θαλάσσῃ, ἀλλ᾽ ὁ λαὸς οὐκ
εἶχεν ἀργύριον αὐτῷ.   8. ὁ διδάσκαλος ὃς ἐστιν ἄξιος τῆς τιμῆς
πιστευέτω τῷ βιβλίῳ καὶ προσκυνείτω τῷ Θεῷ.   9. ἐστιν καινὸς

καιρος τοις λοιποις οἳ μενουσιν.   10. αἱ παρθενοι αἳ ἠσθιον τον
ἀρτον οὐκ ἐκρινον ἑαυτας.   11. ὑποκριτα, μετανοει και μισει τας
ἁμαρτιας ἁς ποιεις.   12. νεανια, ἀκουε τας ἐπαγγελιας ἁς ποιω
τῃ ἰδιᾳ γλωσσῃ.   13. λαμβανετωσαν την διδαχην της καινης
διαθηκης και μαρτυρειτωσαν τῃ μονῃ κεφαλῃ της αἰωνιου βασιλειας.
14. οἱ μικροι μη εἰσιν ἰσχυροι;   15. ὀλιγος οἰνος οὐκ ἐστιν ἱκανος
ἀπιστῳ γενεᾳ;   16. ἠκολουθουν ἁμαρτωλοις, ἠσαν γαρ ὁμοιοι
προβατοις.

19A

1. Take hold of me, people of Judaea, and save yourselves from this
evil generation.   2. They were serving you and were binding themselves to your eternal covenant.   3. We were building houses for
you outside the village beside the river.   4. My sheep hear my word
and keep it.   5. Your word is truth.   6. For I am not only weak
(ill), but I am dying daily.   7. He reads the book, but I obey it.
8. We were recognising the truth, but they were persecuting the
faithful.   9. And I offer sacrifices, which God receives.   10. But
my house was a house of prayer.   11. And that man marries the
happy virgin.   12. You are bearing witness concerning yourself.
Your witness is unclean.   13. But I was not speaking from myself.
14. And I am in the midst of you as a servant.   15. Do not do your
righteousness before men, as the hypocrites do in the synagogues.
16. You are not of (from) the world as I am not of (from) the world.
17. The teacher who is not with me is against me.   18. Some persuade, some only exhort.

19B

1. Ἡμεις μεν ἐφωνουμεν και ἐκλαιομεν, ὑμεις δε οὐκ ἠλεειτε ἡμας.
2. ἐμοι μεν ἐδοκει σοφον, οἱ δε ἠκολουθουν ἑτερᾳ ὁδῳ.   3. Κυριε,
ἐλεει ἡμας καθ’ ἡμεραν ἀχρι (ἑως) της δευτερας παρουσιας σου.   4. ἡ
ἐμη διδαχη οὐκ ἐστιν ἐμη.   5. κρατουσιν τον Ἰησουν και ἀδικουσιν
αὐτον. 6. ὁ δε ἐλεγεν, Ὑποκριτα, ὑπαγε ἀπ’ ἐμου. 7. τουτο δε ἐστιν
το σημειον της σης παρουσιας.   8. ἡ προσευχη ποιειται ὑπ’ ἐμου και
ὑπο του λαου σου.   9. φιλεις τον ἐχθρον σου (τον σον ἐχθρον) ὡς σεαυ-
τον.   10. τουτο λεγεις περι σεαυτου;   11. κἀγω ἐχω ὑπ’ ἐμαυτον

στρατιωτας. 12. οὐκ εἰμι ὥσπερ οἱ λοιποι των ἀνθρωπων. 13. καθως ἀκουω κρινω. 14. φιλειτε ἀλληλους ὡς ὑμας φιλω. 15. ὁ δε
λεγει ἡμιν, Προσφερετε τους πτωχους προς με. 16. οἱ μεν ἀπελυον-
το, οἱ δε ἀπεθνησκον. 17. αἱ δε προσευχαι ὑμων ἀκουονται.
18. οἱ μεν ἠσαν δουλοι, οἱ δε ἐλευθεροι.

20 A

1. They were wishing to persecute us until the last hour.　　2. The
clouds depart and the souls of men wish to give thanks.　　3. I am
about to persuade the worthy elders to dwell apart from sinners.
4. Were you able to have wise friends?　　5. Teacher, it is necessary
for us to believe; *or*, we must believe.　　6. We therefore were wishing
to heal their sons.　　7. Is it lawful for us to receive the kingdom of
heaven?　　8. He was sending his slaves to call the poor and the blind.
9. For God sends his son to save the world.　　10. We were exhorting
the people to obey the prophets.　　11. And the crowds rejoiced when
they heard and saw the signs which he was doing.　　12. Before they
departed Peter used to eat with them.　　13. And because unrighteousness abounds does love die?　　14. The wind was strong so that it was
throwing the boat upon the rocks.　　15. But to walk in his ways is
good for the sons of men.　　16. But the young men remained before
the door of the temple because the elder was dying.　　17. I do not
hate my enemy, with the result that I can love God.　　18. I was
writing in order that you might perceive my love.　　19. I am receiving
the gospel in order that I may be saved.　　20. For you need us to
teach you the truth.

20 B

1. Κακοι δε δυνανται εὑρισκειν την σοφιαν;　　2. οὐκ ἠθελεν
ἀπολυεσθαι ἀπο της ἁμαρτιας;　　3. οὐκ ἠθελον ὑπακουειν τοις
πρεσβυτεροις.　　4. μη ἐξεστιν αὐτοις λαμβανειν το ἀργυριον ἀπο
των τελωνων;　　5. ἐγω μεν εἰμι ἀνθρωπος, ὑμεις δε τεκνα ἐστε.
6. θελομεν θεωρειν το ἱερον του Θεου Ἰσραηλ.　　7. πεμπομεν τους
δουλους καλειν τους τυφλους και τους πτωχους.　　8. ἐδει τον
Ἰησουν ἀπαγειν τους μαθητας ἀπο της Γαλιλαιας.　　9. ἠθελον

αὐτον θεραπευειν το τεκνον μου, ὁ δε οὐκ ἠθελεν.   10. ὁ Ἰησους
μελλει αἰτειν αὐτους πεμπειν ἱκανον ἀρτον.   11. οὐ δυναμαι
παρακαλειν αὐτους εὐχαριστειν ὑπερ της παρουσιας του της Δικαιοσυνης Ἡλιου.   12. (μητι) δυναμεθα ποιειν τουτο;   13. ἐπεμπον
τον ἀγγελον προς ὑμας, ὁ δε οὐκ ἠθελεν ὑπαγειν.   14. θελουσιν
ἀναγινωσκειν τα βιβλια ἁ ἐχεις.   15. ὁ δε λαος ἐπιστευεν τον
Ἰωανην προφητην εἰναι.   16. ἐν δε τῳ συναγεσθαι τους πρεσβυτερους ἐμενομεν ἐν τοις ἀγροις. 17. και ὁ Ἰησους ἐθεραπευεν τους
πτωχους, ὡστε τον ὀχλον χαιρειν.   18. παρεκαλουν δε τον Πετρον
δια το αὐτον διδασκειν τας ἐντολας.   19. εἰχεν δε τα ἱματια εἰς
(προς) το αὐτην εἰναι καλην.

21 A

1. Will they not injure the children?   2. But will you call the child
Peter?   3. And he will open the eyes of the blind who are being
gathered together in the synagogue.   4. I will send to them wise men
and prophets, but the children (sons) of Israel will not hear them.
5. You will prophesy to this people and they will obey you.   6. The
servants of the synagogue will not pursue the young men on the
Sabbath.   7. The lepers will have the sheep which are being saved
from the winds and the sea.   8. But they will put the clothes on the
widows.   9. And when the crowd was hearing the word, the demons
used to bring sacrifices to offer them to Satan.   10. For I wish to
remain with you this day before I follow Jesus in the way of the cross.
11. But the tree was weak, because it had no earth.   12. They are
therefore sending him to his friends to bless God with them.   13. Is
it not the time to believe?   14. Therefore he calls to us daily to
encourage us.   15. And you have authority to walk in Galilee.

21 B

1. Ἀνοιξω τα βιβλια ἁ ἐστιν ἐν τῃ συναγωγῃ.   2. θεωρησομεν το
προσωπον του Κυριου ἐν τῳ ἱερῳ ὁ οἰκοδομειται ἐν τοις Ἱεροσολυμοις.   3. πεμψομεν τους δουλους διωκειν αὐτους ἀχρι της Ἰου-
δαιας.   4. λαλησει ταυτα τοις ὀχλοις ἐν παραβολαις.   5. μη
εὐλογειτε (τους) πονηρους, οἱ γαρ πονηροι οὐ βλεψουσιν τον ἡλιον.
6. μελλετε ἀλληλοις πιστευειν;   7. πεισομεν ἀρα τους ἰδιους

ἀδελφοὺς ἐκβάλλειν τοὺς δεξιοὺς ὀφθαλμοὺς (αὐτῶν); 8. καὶ
καλεσουσιν τὸ τεκνον Ἰησουν, σωζει γαρ τον λαον αὐτου ἀπο των
ἁμαρτιων αὐτων. (With a name after καλεω there is no article, cf.
21 A2, Matt. 1. 21.) 9. ἑξει δε φωνην ὁμοιαν τῃ φωνῃ ἀγγελου.
10. προ δε του τον κοσμον εἰναι, ἐγω εἰμι. 11. μη ποιειτε την
δικαιοσυνην ὑμων προς το τους ἀνθρωπους βλεπειν.

22 A

1. And I will draw near to each beloved brother. 2. Hope in God,
for he will open a door for you in your need. 3. Cleanse your own
hearts and you will walk before me in ways of joy. 4. Hide your face
from my sins. 5. And the poor man will cry out in the middle of the
temple. 6. We will carry the paralysed man to the door, and they
will prepare to receive him. 7. The rest, who are wondering at his
authority, will proclaim his love. 8. And I will draw near as far as
the first tomb. 9. He sits upon the throne of heaven, but the saints
will hope to see his coming on the clouds. 10. Proclaim the promises
and guard the commandments as (while) you prepare the way of
glory.

22 B

1. Ἡ πιστη χηρα καθισει ἐν (τῃ) προσευχῃ και ἡ μαρτυρια
αὐτης οὐ σκανδαλισει τας ἀλλας. 2. ἐλεησει με, και ἑξω (την)
αἰωνιον σωτηριαν. 3. ἀγοραζετε τας θυσιας ὑμων και ἀγιαζετε το
σαββατον. 4. οἱ μαθηται οὑς ὁ Ἰωανης ἐβαπτιζεν μετα του
Ἰησου ἐμενον. 5. οὐκ ἀποκαλυψει το προσωπον αὐτου τῃ
ἀπιστῳ ψυχῃ; 6. οἱ λεπροι κραξουσιν ἐν τῃ χρειᾳ αὐτων. 7. ὁ
μεν διαβολος πειρασει ὑμας, ἐγω δε φυλαξω ὑμας. 8. πρασσετε
την δικαιοσυνην ἀλληλοις και δοξασετε τον μονον Θεον. 9. ὠ
Πετρε, πειρασω σε και πονηροι θαυμασουσιν την ὑπομονην σου.
10. ἀγορασεις ἀρα τα ἱματια και βαστασεις αὐτα εἰς τους ἀδελφους;
11. και ἀποκαλυψω την ἁμαρτιαν των ἀνθρωπων οἱ πρασσουσιν την
ἀδικιαν, και κρυψουσιν τους ὀφθαλμους (αὐτων) ἀπ᾽ ἐμου.

23 A

1. And we were going to the sea with the disciples. 2. Were they, then, denying the Lord who keeps them from the evil one? 3. Do not answer the voice. 4. For they were going away to the desert in which John himself was baptising. 5. And I used to answer the messengers who came from the elders. 6. Do not work unrighteousness. 7. And he (that man) receives (the) sinners who come to him and eats with them. 8. Touch (take hold of) the heads of the children whom I send. 9. Not even the strong slaves whom he used to receive work only. 10. Let him first receive the book which the apostle is writing. 11. Therefore we were going through their fields and were following after the second tax-collector. 12. Let them take hold of the new stones of the third temple which is being built for the Lord. 13. But they were wishing to hear the last words which Jesus was speaking. 14. This man begins to build, but is not able to do the work. 15. You must answer this generation. 16. I command you to come out of the house. 17. For are you not about to come to me? 18. But he did not wish to go in the ways of truth. 19. This man was a ruler of the synagogue. 20. I have no silver; but what I have, I offer. 21. Christ himself will rule the church, and his people will pray and preach the gospel. 22. Greet one another with joy. 23. God will reckon righteousness to him apart from works. 24. And they were coming and were being baptised by John. 25. And the first comes to his lord. 26. Do not fear the remaining enemies, only believe. 27. You will not even become men of anger. 28. For she will be powerful before the whole people. 29. For it is necessary to put on the new man.

23 B

1. Λογιζεσθε ἑαυτους εἰναι νεκρους. 2. γενησομαι δυνατος φιλος ὁμοιος τῳ πλουσιῳ; 3. ὁ πονηρος ἀρχων ἐφοβειτο τον Ἰωανην. 4. ἡ ἐκκλησια γινεται ὁμοια καλῃ παρθενῳ, ἡν ὁ Θεος ἑτοιμαζει εἰς (την) ζωην (την) αἰωνιον. 5. ἐσεσθε δε ἁγιοι τῳ Κυριῳ. 6. λημψομεθα οὐν το ποτηριον της σωτηριας μετα χαρας. 7. κἀγω

γνωσομαι ὡς αὐτος γινωσκει.   8. ἐβουλομεθα πορευεσθαι και
ἀσπαζεσθαι ὑμας, ὁ δε βουλεται ὑμας ἐρχεσθαι και προσευχεσθαι
μεθ' ἡμων.   9. γενησομαι δε σοφος και (προσ)ελευσομαι προς
αὐτον (αὐτῳ) (ἐν) τῳ φοβῳ του Κυριου.   10. μη ἀδικησει τον ἰδιον
δεξιον ὀφθαλμον;   11. και τηρειτε τας ἁγιας ἐντολας ἁς δεχεσθε
ἀπο των διδασκαλων.   12. μη ἀρνεισθε τον Κυριον της δοξης ὁς
σωσει ὑμας ἀπο του πονηρου κοσμου.   13. διηρχομεθα δε τους
ἀγρους (or, δια των ἀγρων) ἐν οἷς οἱ δουλοι ἡργαζοντο.   14. δεχε-
σθω τους ἀγγελους οἳ κηρυσσουσιν την βασιλειαν των οὐρανων.
15. ἀδελφοι, μη ἀποκρινεσθε τῳ διδασκαλῳ.   16. οἱ μεν ἡρχοντο
εἰς τους οἰκους αὐτων, οἱ δε εἰς το ἱερον.   17. ὁ Ἰησους ἀγεται εἰς
την αὐτην ἐρημον πειραζεσθαι ὑπο του διαβολου.   18. ἐπορευομεθα
δε προς τον Ἰωανην βαπτιζεσθαι ὑπ' αὐτου.   19. ὁ Ἰησους οὐν
ἠρχετο πεμπειν τους ἀποστολους εὐαγγελιζεσθαι ὁλῳ τῳ οἰκῳ
(or, ὁλον τον οἰκον) Ἰσραηλ.   20. ἐγω μεν ἐσομαι πρωτος, συ δε
ἐσῃ ἐσχατος.

24A

1. They did not even pursue the tax-collectors who were leading away
the sheep.   2. But did the lepers believe the word of Jesus?   3. For
you sent the widows to buy the clothes.   4. Save the silver from her.
5. Save your people (*i.e.*, keep them safe continually) from the evil one.
6. After this (these things) we persuaded them to hide the children.
7. Therefore we cleansed ourselves in the river.   8. And the teacher
himself wondered at the wisdom of his own disciples.   9. But do
they wish to injure the honour of the rest?   10. Carry the other boat
from the sea.   11. Sanctify yourselves, for the day of the Lord is
drawing near.   12. For the voice of John cried out in the desert,
Prepare the way for the Lord.   13. And we kept the commandments
which we heard from the believing soldiers.   14. It is good for us to
practise righteousness.   15. After this each (one) opened the eyes of a
blind man.   16. For the angels wished to see these things.   17. And
they put his clothes on him.

24B

1. Ἐβαπτισαν δε τους τελωνας ἐν τῳ ποταμῳ.   2. διηρχεσθε την
καλην γην ἑτοιμασαι τον ἐλευθερον λαον.   3. ἐργατα ἰσχυρε,
κρυψον τους λιθους οἳ περισσευουσιν ἐν τῳ ἀγρῳ.   4. μη σκανδαλι-
ζετε τους ἀδελφους οἳ ἠσθενουν.   5. ἠκολουθησαν δε ἀλληλοις.
6. ἀπεκαλυψατε γαρ τας ἐντολας και τας ἐπαγγελιας τῃ ἐκκλησιᾳ.
7. ἀρξομεθα ἀναγινωσκειν τα βιβλια;   8. καθαρισατε και ἁγιασατε
τας καρδιας ὑμων.   9. ἐξεστιν αὐτοις θεραπευειν ἐν τῳ σαββατῳ;
10. σωζε τον λαον σου, Κυριε, ἀπο της ἀδικιας του κοσμου τουτου.
11. κρυψατε οὐν ἑαυτους και τα τεκνα ὑμων ἐν τοις Ἱεροσολυμοις.
12. κατοικειτωσαν ἡ ἀγαπη και ἡ εἰρηνη και ἡ δικαιοσυνη τας
καρδιας (or, ἐν ταις καρδιαις) ὑμων.   13. ὁ δε ἐχθρος αὐτης
ἐθαυμασεν την ὑπομονην αὐτης.   14. καλον ἐστιν αὐτους τα αὐτα
ἀναγινωσκειν.   15. μετα ταυτα (or, τουτο) την ἐξουσιαν μου και
τας χρειας μου ἀποκαλυψω αὐτοις.   16. ἠθελησεν καλεσαι τους
τελωνας εἰς την θυσιαν.   17. ἡ δε γλωσσα αὐτου ἠδικησεν ἀλλους.
18. χωρις μου δοκειτε ἀσθενειν.

25A

1. After this the poor man died.   2. We went up to the temple at
that hour.   3. O Lord, I (have) sinned before you (in your sight).
4. Behold, we carried the stones from the sea.   5. The trees did not
even fall into the field.   6. The strong men were fleeing from the
young men.   7. But the prophets fled into the desert.   8. Go
outside the village and take the fruit from the workmen.   9. Let the
children come to me.   10. He had my brother's books.   11. And
I found the money and carried it to them, so that they received their
reward.   12. But he will carry the cross and drink the cup.   13. We
shall take his powerful salvation and shall know his peace.   14. They
will go down to the riverside and will offer a sacrifice.   15. But he
departed and threw it into the sea.   16. And when they brought
the child to offer him to the Lord, the people blessed God.

25 B

1. Ἐβαλομεν οὐν ἑαυτους εἰς τον ποταμον. 2. ἐλαβετε δε τα ἱματια ἁ οἱ πρεσβυτεροι ἐπεμψαν τοις πτωχοις. 3. ἐφυγον ἀρα ἀπο του προσωπου των κριτων; 4. οὑτος ἐστιν ὁ λιθος ὁς ἐπεσεν ἐκ του οὐρανου. 5. ἡ παρθενος ἐσχεν υἱον, και ἐκαλεσαν αὐτον Ἰησουν. 6. δει γαρ τον υἱον του ἀνθρωπου παθειν (πασχειν). 7. μετα ταυτας τας ἡμερας ἠλθομεν εἰς την Γαλιλαιαν. 8. δια τουτο κατελιπον τα προβατα ἐν τοις ἀγροις και ὑπηγον. 9. δει τον ὀχλον φαγειν τον ἀρτον και πιειν τον οἰνον ὁν (οὑς) οἱ αὐτοι νεανιαι ἠνεγκον εἰς αὐτους. 10. ὁ ἑτερος προφητης ὁς ἐσχεν το πρωτον βιβλιον ἀπεθανεν μονος. 11. ἰδε ἐγνω τας καρδιας ἡμων. 12. ἐμαθον γαρ παθειν και ὀψονται το προσωπον αὐτου. 13. κατελιπεν την οἰκιαν και ἐλευσεται εἰς το ἱερον. 14. εἰδομεν δε τον ἡλιον και εἰπομεν λογους της χαρας και της μετανοιας. 15. ἐφαγομεν και ἐπιομεν μετ' αὐτου ἐπι τῃ γῃ και φαγομεθα και πιομεθα μετ' αὐτου ἐν τῳ οὐρανῳ.

26 A

1. But when the soldiers came to the house they announced that he had sent them. 2. Will these men judge the widows and kill their children? 3. You will not remain in this place, but you will die in the land of your enemies. 4. But the apostles sowed the word in the hearts of the few who were willing to obey it. 5. He therefore lifted up the cross and came after Jesus. 6. At that time the judges judged the unbelieving women. 7. But I remained in my own place until he had read the book. 8. Can you drink the cup which I must drink? 9. But we remained in the temple while the workmen were building the throne. 10. But when they heard these things from the widow they remained with her. 11. You were not even owing money to the tax-collectors. 12. But Jesus said to the paralysed man, Lift it up and depart to your house; and when he heard this (these things) he lifted it up and departed. 13. Therefore we sent the messengers to prepare the way. 14. The prophet said, It is possible. He said that it was possible. He said, It is possible. 15. You commanded them not to injure the whole people. 16. And this we

heard from him, that we must (ought to) love our brothers.   17. But
the Pharisees were saying that he was eating with a sinner.   18. And
you will carry the cross after me.   19. And he will say these things
to her because they love one another.   20. You learnt that the strong
judge was coming.   21. They said that they were drinking enough
wine.   22. I knew that the Lord had sent the angel to save me.
23. They saw that we had led the crowd into the same synagogue.

26B

1. Ἀπόστειλον (πέμψον) τοὺς νεανίας ἐγεῖραι τοὺς στρατιώτας.
2. ἔλαβεν δὲ τὸ παιδίον καὶ ὑπῆγεν.   3. οὐκ ἀποθανοῦνται
ἐν τῇ ἐρήμῳ, οἱ γὰρ στρατιῶται σώσουσιν αὐτούς.   4. κρινῶ
οὖν τὸν λαόν μου ἐν ἐκείνῳ τῷ καιρῷ.   5. οἱ δὲ Φαρισαῖοι ἦλθον
φαγεῖν ἄρτον παρὰ τῷ προφήτῃ.   6. καὶ ὅτε ἤκουσεν τοὺς λόγους
τούτους ἀπέστειλεν αὐτοὺς ἀποκτεῖναι τὸν ἐχθρὸν αὐτοῦ.   7. μενοῦσιν ἐν τῇ οἰκίᾳ ἕως ὁ παραλυτικὸς ἀποθνήσκει.   8. ἀπηγγείλα-
μεν οὖν ὅτι ὁ ἀπόστολος ἔπεσεν.   9. τὰς δὲ χήρας ταύτας οὐκ
ὀφείλετε κρῖναι.   10. ἐκβαλεῖ δὲ τὸν δεξιὸν ὀφθαλμὸν (αὐτοῦ) ὅτι
ἀσθενεῖτε.   11. ὅτε οἱ μαθηταὶ ἦλθον εἰς τὴν κώμην ἔσπειραν τὸν
λόγον ἐν ταῖς καρδίαις τοῦ λαοῦ.   12. οὐκ ἀποκτενεῖς τοὺς
πονηρούς, ὦ Κύριε;   13. βαλεῖτε τοὺς λίθους παρὰ τὸ ἱερόν.
14. οἱ δὲ Φαρισαῖοι εἶπον ὅτι οἱ μαθηταὶ τοῦ Ἰωάνου οὐκ ἐσθίουσιν
παρὰ τελώναις καὶ ἁμαρτωλοῖς.   15. πεσοῦμαι ἀλλ' οὐκ ἀποθανοῦ-
μαι ὅτι ἐγερεῖς με.   16. καὶ ἐροῦσιν ὅτι Ἀπέθανεν ἐν τῇ πρώτῃ
ἡμέρᾳ ἕως ἠργαζόμεθα.

27A

1. You denied the holy and righteous man privately, but he denied him
before the whole people.   2. The widow only took hold of (touched)
his garment, but he said, Do not touch (continue to hold) me.   3. He
greeted them, but they began to beseech him to go away.   4. Heaven
must receive him, but we shall see him on the day of his second coming.
5. And he answered, Preach the gospel to him.   6. And I reckon him
a friend, for he worked a good work on my behalf.   7. His disciples
therefore began to make a way.   8. But the first came and said, Lord,

we wish to learn to pray. 9. Let the elder be as the deacon (servant). 10. And it came to pass while they were in the house, the wise men came to Jerusalem. 11. And that man perished, but his sons did not perish. 12. You began from the last until the first. 13. Therefore be wise towards one another. 14. He put on no garment and he used not to remain in the house. 15. And it came to pass as he sowed others fell beside the way.

27 B

1. Ἠρξατο δε ὁ Ἰησους λεγειν τοις ὀχλοις περι Ἰωανου ὁτι Ἡτοιμασεν την ὁδον μου. 2. ἀνθρωπος ἀρνησασθω ἑαυτον και ἐλθετω (ἐρχεσθω) ὀπισω μου. 3. Πετρε, ἐλθε εἰς την οἰκιαν της ἀπιστου και ἀσπασαι αὐτην. 4. ἐν δε τῃ ἡμερᾳ ἐκεινῃ οἱ λοιποι ἁγιοι εὐηγγελισαντο (-ζοντο) και ἠργασαντο (-ζοντο) δικαιοσυνην. 5. ἀνεβη δε εἰς το ἱερον προσευξασθαι. 6. ἁμαρτωλε, δεξαι τον λογον μετα φοβου. 7. μη γινεσθε ὡς οἱ ὑποκριται (or, ὁμοιοι τοις ὑποκριταις), ἀλλα γινεσθε πιστοι ἀλληλοις (or προς ἀλληλους). 8. και ἐγενετο ἐν τῳ σπειρειν τα σπερματα ἐπεσεν παρα την ὁδον. 9. ἐν τῳ κοσμῳ ἠν, και ὁ κοσμος δι' αὐτου ἐγενετο, και ὁ κοσμος αὐτον οὐκ ἐγνω. 10. οὐκ ἐξεστιν προφητην ἀπολεσθαι ἐξω των Ἱεροσολυμων. 11. Πετρε, μη γινου ἀπιστος.

28 A

1. For we are being saved by hope and by the grace of God. 2. And you are being raised by the hands of the woman. 3. Let the children be guarded by the Greeks. 4. And the rulers sent the soldiers by night. 5. The same men therefore lifted up (took away) the image of Simon. 6. Will they not remain in their land for ever? 7. In the first month you took the fruit of the vineyard for the wives of the other witnesses. 8. The blind father loved his daughter. 9. Behold, O woman, the stars of heaven bear witness to the Saviour. 10. For you will eat the flesh of the Son of man. 11. And he killed her with the feet of the image which fell in the middle of the sanctuary. 12. But the reward is not reckoned according to grace. 13. Therefore a man must leave his father and mother. 14. After his father died he dwelt in this land.

28B

1. Γυναι, μη εὑρες ἱκανον ἀργυριον τοις ἀρχουσιν; 2. αὐτος δε ὁ διδασκαλος ἐπεμψεν τους ἰδιους παιδας εἰς τον ἀμπελωνα. 3. ἀλλ' ἡ νυξ και ἡ ἡμερα οὐ μενοῦσιν εἰς τους αἰωνας των αἰωνων. 4. μετα ταυτα ἐθεωρησαμεν τον ἀστερα μετ' αὐτων. 5. ἀπηγγειλαμεν δε ὁτι ἐστιν σωτηρ (ταις) γυναιξιν. 6. αὐτων ἡ σαρξ ἀσθενει, ἀλλ' οἱ μαρτυρες σωζονται τῃ χαριτι. 7. ἠργασαντο δε ταις χερσιν και τοις ποσιν. 8. ὁ σωτηρ ἐστιν ὑπερ τον διδασκαλον, ὁτι ἀπεθανεν ὑπερ των προβατων. 9. ἀλλα καλαι θυγατερες γενησονται ὁμοιαι ταις μητρασιν αὐτων. 10. ἐν τῳ ἐσχατῳ μηνι περισσευσει ἡ ἐλπις. 11. δια τουτο οἰσουσιν την εἰκονα δια του ἱερου. 12. χωρις της σαρκος του υἱου οὐχ ἑξυμεν (την) αἰωνιον ζωην ἐν ἑαυτοις. 13. ὁτι ἡ παις ἐστιν ὑπο ἐξουσιαν, οὐ πειραζεται ὑπο του διαβολου. 14. ὁτι οὐκ ἐσμεν ὑπο νομον ἀλλ' ὑπο χαριν. 15. ὁ ἀνηρ και ἡ γυνη εἰσιν ἡ αὐτη σαρξ.

29A

1. But I wish mercy and not sacrifice. 2. And the enemies of Judah killed part of the nation with fire. 3. Shall we then have a baptism of repentance through his blood? 4. And he will do signs and wonders for our race. 5. But the children took the vessels out of the water. 6. But strong words of judgement came out of your mouth. 7. For I did not come to do my will, but the will of the Lord who sent me. 8. Therefore he comes in mercy to the members of his body. 9. And the Gentiles will know his name. 10. After this (these things) he touched the ear with his hand. 11. The water abounds in the vessels. 12. The words of his mouth were for the ears of the Gentiles (nations). 13. According to his mercy he saved us.

29B

1. Ἀλλα ὁ Θεος ἐστιν πλουσιος ἐν ἐλεει. 2. εἰπεν οὐν ὁτι οὐκ ἐστιν (αὐτος) ῥο φως, ἀλλ' ἐρχεται μαρτυρησαι περι του φωτος. 3. και διηλθομεν δια πυρος και ὑδατος, το γαρ πνευμα (του) ἐλεους

κατῳκει ἡμας (ἐν ἡμιν).   4. ἀνοιξει δε τα ὠτα των πληθων ἁ οὐ
δυναται ἀκουειν.   5. οὐδε τα ἐτη των ὁρων ἐσται εἰς τον αἰωνα·
το γαρ τελος σκοτος του κριματος ἐσται.   6. αὐτοι δε ἐσμεν μελη
του σωματος αὐτου.   7. δει γαρ το σπερμα του Ἀβρααμ φαγειν το
πασχα.   8. ἰδετε τας χειρας και τους ποδας μου.   9. ἐστιν ἡ
ὁδος (του) φωτος τοις πληθεσιν.   10. και ἐρουσιν τοις ὁρεσιν,
Πεσετε ἐφ' ἡμας.   11. και ἐσται τερατα ἐν τῳ σκοτει της νυκτος,
αἱμα και πυρ και φοβος.   12. το δε τελος της ὁδου φως του
Πνευματος ἐσται.   13. ἀλλ', ἀπιστε γυναι, εἰπες ὁτι γινωσκεις το
θελημα του Θεου.   14. και πραξουσιν τερατα ἐν τῳ ὀνοματι
αὐτου.   15. ἐβαλεν δε το σπερμα εἰς σκευος ἐν τῃ ἡμερᾳ του πασχα.
16. οἱ ἀρα Ἰουδαιοι ἐγενοντο μερος ὁλου του γενους.   17. μη
δυνανται οἱ ποδες εἰπειν ταις χερσιν ὁτι Χρειαν ὑμων οὐκ ἐχομεν,
ὁτι οὐκ ἐστε μελη του σωματος;   18. το δε Ἁγιον Πνευμα
μενει μετ' αὐτων εἰς τους αἰωνας των αἰωνων.   19. ὁ δε κοσμος
ὑδατι ἀπωλετο.

30A

1. He sent a better covenant which is in the blood of the Saviour.
2. And am I not greater than he?   3. And Jesus departed full of the
Holy Spirit.   4. Abraham, your righteousness abounds, because it is
more than the righteousness of your race.   5. Why was his witness
not true? The flesh is weak.   6. Say, Who is worthy in the village
itself?   7. But your brother has something against you.   8. And
certain of the Pharisees said in themselves, Why does he blaspheme?
9. For whoever has will receive more.   10. What does it seem to you
(what do you think), Simon? Who do you say that I am?   11. Is
anyone able to go into the house of the strong man?   12. Because he
is the wise man who built his own house upon the same rock.   13. The
last state of the man becomes worse than the first.

30B

1. Παραλημψονται δε μισθον ὁς ἐστιν κρεισσων (της) ζωης.
2. ὁ ἀρα Χριστος ἐστιν μειζων του ἱερου.   3. ἠν γαρ ἀνθρωπος
πληρης (της) χαριτος και (της) ἀληθειας.   4. οἱ πρωτοι ἐργαται

εἶπον ὅτι Παραλημψομεθα πλειονα τιμην.   5. οἱ δε ἀληθεις
πρεσβυτεροι ἐν ἐλεει παρακαλουσιν τα ἀσθενη παιδια αὑτων.
6. ὅστις θελει ὀπισω μου ἐλθειν, ἀρνησασθω ἑαυτον.   7. ἁγιος τις
ἀπεθανεν και οὐ κατελιπεν παιδια.   8. ὅτε γαρ ἠμεν ἐν τῃ σαρκι
δουλοι ἠμεν της ἁμαρτιας.   9. οὑτοι εἰσιν οἱ ἀνθρωποι οἱτινες
(οἳ) ἀκουουσιν τα ῥηματα του πληθους.   10. οὑτος μη ἐστιν
χειρων ᾿Ιουδα;   11. τί με πειραζεις, ὑποκριτα; τίνος ἐστιν ἡ
εἰκων αὑτη;   12. λαλουσιν τινες κατα σαρκα, ἀλλα το Πνευμα
ἐστιν κατα της σαρκος.

31A

1. Behold, you are being sought by your mother and your brothers.
2. And the men were walking in the cities with their wives.   3. Therefore he commanded his own daughters to prepare the fish for the king.
4. I baptise you with water, but he will baptise us with power.
5. These are the men who say there is no resurrection.   6. For I did
not receive it from man, but by revelation.   7. Do you wish (for)
faith and a good conscience?   8. And there will be a worse time of
judgement and tribulation.   9. For the disciple does not love father
and mother more than me.   10. Why don't they walk according to
the traditions of the priests?   11. But that man has not forgiveness
for ever (never has forgiveness).   12. And tribulation will come
because of the word.

31B

1. Και δει τους γραμματεις λαβειν τους ἰχθυας ἐκ του ὑδατος τοις
ἱερευσιν.   2. τῃ δε πιστει αὐτου ἀνοιξει τα ὠτα του πατρος αὐτης.
3. και ἐθαυμαζον ὅτι μετα του ἀρχιερεως ἐλαλει.   4. οἱ γαρ
ἀνδρες εἶπον ὅτι εἶδον την θυγατερα του βασιλεως.   5. ἐν
τῃ ἀναστασει τίνος ἐσται γυνη;   6. ἡ δε γνωσις μου του μυστηριου
ἠλθεν κατ᾿ ἀποκαλυψιν.   7. αἱ δε των ἀνθρωπων παραδοσεις οὐκ
ἀξουσιν την ἀφεσιν των ἁμαρτιων.   8. οὐκ ἐγνωτε την δυναμιν και
την χαριν του Θεου;   9. οἱ γαρ πατερες ἡμων ἐπερισσευον (ἐν)
πιστει και (ἐν) γνωσει.   10. και διωξουσιν ὑμας ἀπο πολεως εἰς
πολιν.   11. αἱ δε συνειδησεις αὐτων ἠσαν ἀσθενεις.   12. ὁ δε
πιστος οὐκ ἐρχεται εἰς κρισιν.

32 A

1. And you will receive all this authority and the glory of the kingdoms.
2. The four robbers fled into the mountains.   3. My name will be great among all the Gentiles.   4. Does no one wish to drink this wine?
5. The six priests came by night and took away the bodies of the three prophets.   6. And every city had twelve gates and all the multitude was rejoicing.   7. O woman, your faith is great.   8. And we know that these ten words are true, because the Lord spoke them by the mouth of Moses.   9. And they did not know until the great flood came and took them all away.   10. Let one of the slaves be sent to sow the seed in the three fields.   11. And many were coming together from the seven villages, and were carrying those who were ill, and were putting them at his feet.   12. Let no one cause one of these children to stumble.   13. But his two parents did not know that he was remaining in the city.   14. Did not the scripture say that the Christ was coming of the seed of David?   15. And at that hour many of the chief priests, who say that there will be no resurrection, gather together to him.   16. With the Lord one day is as a thousand years.
17. But the centurion answered, I am a man under authority and I have a hundred soldiers under me.   18. And the number of the men was about five thousand.   19. And he talked to two of them.

32 B

1. Οὐδεὶς οὖν δύναται δυο κυριους ἐχειν.   2. ἀνοιξεις δε τα στοματα ἡμων, Κυριε, και πασα γλωσσα εὐλογησει το μεγα ὀνομα σου.
3. οὐκ ἐσπειρας καλον σπερμα ἐν τοις τρισιν ἀγροις;   4. μη βασταζετε μηδενα εἰς την συναγωγην ἐν τῳ σαββατῳ.   5. δυνασαι δε θεραπευσαι τον χιλιαρχον.   6. ἠλθον δε εἰς τον κοσμον τουτον εἰς μεγαλην κρισιν.   7. εἰς δε των λεπρων, ὁτε εἰδεν ὁτι θεραπευεται, ἐβαλεν ἑαυτον παρα τους ποδας αὐτου.
8. οἱ γαρ ἀρχιερεις ἐγνωσαν ὁτι το ῥημα τουτο ἀληθες ἐστιν.
9. και παντες οἱ μαθηται πληρεις πιστεως ἠσαν και του Ἁγιου Πνευματος, και ἐθεραπευσαν (ἐθεραπευον) τους ἀσθενεις και ἐξεβαλον (ἐξεβαλλον) πολλα δαιμονια.   10. οὐδεις των ἱερεων

30

πιστευει ὁτι ἀναστασις ἐστιν.   11. οἱ φιλοι μου ᾠκοδομησαν
μεγαν οἰκον ἐν τῃ πολει ταυτῃ.   12. ἡ κρισις μου ἀληθης ἐστιν·
μηδεις φιλειτω το σκοτος.   13. ὁτε ἠλθον εἰς τας ἐξ κωμας
ἐκηρυξαν το εὐαγγελιον πασιν τοις ἐθνεσιν ἁ κατῳκει (or, using
construction according to sense, οἱ κατῳκουν) αὐτας (or ἐν αὐταις).
14. ὁτε οἱ μαθηται του Ἰωανου ἠκουσαν ὁτι ἀπεθανεν ἐν ἐκεινῃ
τῃ ἡμερᾳ, ἠλθον και ἠραν το σωμα αὐτου.   15. ἐχομεν δε
μονον δυο ἀρτους και πεντε ἰχθυας.   16. και ἐξηλθεν νυκτος προς
τον οἰκον Ἰουδα, ἑνος των δωδεκα.   17. ἑκατον δε ἀνδρες συν ταις
γυναιξιν αὐτων μενουσιν ἐν τῃ μεγαλῃ ἐρημῳ τεσσαρακοντα ἡμερας
και τεσσαρακοντα νυκτας.   18. ὁ χιλιαρχος και χιλιοι ἀνδρες
κατῳκουν ἐν ταις τρισιν πολεσιν (or, τας τρεις πολεις).   19. οὐδεις
δυναται δυσιν κυριοις ἀκολουθειν.

33A

1. Alas, is not the soul more (a greater thing) than food?   2. Let the
one who is greater among you become as the younger.   3. For now is
our salvation nearer than when we believed.   4. Truly this man was
the Son of God.   5. But he that is least in the kingdom of heaven is
greater than he.   6. And now there remain faith, hope, love, these
three; but the greatest of these is love.   7. Yes, he who is stronger
than I comes after me.   8. You will see greater things than these.
9. But they cried out the more (lit. more greatly), Lord, have mercy
upon us.   10. All the disciples also said similarly.   11. For that
which fills it up takes away from the garment and a worse tear is made.
12. Truly I say to you, When you did (it) to one of the least of these my
brothers, you did it to me.   13. Will he say the Amen to your
thanksgiving?   14. It is necessary to obey God rather than men.
15. I say to you, There is no one greater than John among those born of
women; but he that is smallest in the kingdom of God is greater than he.
16. For I am the least of the apostles.   17. The foolishness of God
is wiser than men, and the weakness of God is stronger than men.
18. God, who is the saviour of all men, especially of believers.

33B

1. Ὁ νεωτερος των υἱων οὐκ ἠθελεν (ἠθελησεν) ἐργαζεσθαι ὑπερ του πατρος αὐτου.   2. οὐαι σοι, ὑποκριτα, πορευου και συ ποιει ὁμοιως.   3. οἱ ἐχθροι αὐτων πλειονες αὐτων ἠσαν.   4. ἰσχυροτερος γαρ ἐστιν παντων των βασιλεων της γης.   5. τί ἐρχῃ εἰς τα Ἱεροσολυμα; ὁ Ἰησους μη ἐστιν μειζων του Ἀβρααμ;   6. ἰδου ἡ ἐλπις και ἡ ἀγαπη μειζονες εἰσιν της πιστεως, μαλιστα ἡ ἀγαπη.   7. οὑτος ὁ ἀγαθος (ἀνθρωπος) ἐποιει (ἐποιησεν) καλως παντα.   8. δει ἡμας ὑπακουειν τῳ βασιλει μαλλον ἠ τῳ ἱερει.   9. λεγουσιν ὁτι αὑται αἱ ἡμεραι εἰσιν χειρονες ἠ αἱ ἡμεραι (των ἡμερων) των πατερων.   10. ναι, ἀπεκτεινατε τον σοφωτατον (-τερον) των ἀνθρωπων.   11. ὁ μικροτερος γενησεται ὁ μειζων.   12. ὁ δε ἐκραξεν μαλλον, Ἰδου πασχω ταις χερσιν των ἐχθρων μου.   13. ἀληθως ἐπιγινωσκω ὁτι ἐστιν χειρον σκοτος τουτου.   14. οὐ δυναμεθα το ἐλαχιστον (μικροτερον) τουτων ποιειν.   15. Ἀμην λεγω ὑμιν ὁτι Πολλοι προφηται ἠθελον (ἠθελησαν) ἰδειν ταυτα.   16. ὁ δε ἀπεκρινατο αὐτοις σοφωτερον του πατρος αὐτου.

34A

1. Children, it is the last hour, and as you heard that Antichrist comes, even now many antichrists have come (into being).   2. If then I have done anything worthy of death.   3. Is it not written, My house is a house of prayer?   4. And the good news has been announced in all the world.   5. Because you have been led into sin.   6. But the weak women have lifted up their voices.   7. And a new revelation has been received by us all.   8. For the Gentiles have gone up to Jerusalem.   9. But this whole people has been known by God from the beginning.   10. Christ, together with all the members of his body, has been raised from the dead.   11. But the four scribes have found all the large vessels.   12. My beloved daughter is dead. She died at the third hour of the night.   13. As far as the mountain on which their city had been built.   14. If you had known the word which is written, I wish for mercy and not sacrifice.   15. They announced my coming, but you did not hear.   16. And my ears have

been opened to his word.   17. Mary, from whom he had cast out seven demons.   18. And they were men who had committed murder. 19. The man upon whom this sign had been done (come to pass). 20. The Lord in whom they had believed.   21. John the Baptist has cried aloud in the desert.   22. But concerning the dead that they are raised, have you not read in the book of Moses how God said to him...? 23. But concerning that day no one knows.   24. Because they knew him to be the Christ.   25. And I wish you to know that the head of every man is Christ.   26. And it comes to pass that he was sitting at table in his house, and many tax-collectors and sinners were sitting at table with Jesus.   27. And he was sitting at table with the twelve disciples.   28. And a very great crowd gathers together[1] to him, so that he sits in a boat in the sea.   29. And Peter was sitting among (in the middle of) them.   30. For all knew that his father was a Greek.   31. For they know that he is dead.   32. And God has spoken these words so that you may know what is the hope of his calling.   33. This man could have been released if he had not[2] appealed to Caesar.   34. No one could bind him, because he had often-been bound.   35. And a certain poor man, Lazarus by name, had been put at his gateway.   36. See the place where the body lay.

34B

1. Οὐκ ἠδίκηκεν σε ἡ τους φιλους σου.   2. Ἰουδα, δει σε κηρυσσειν ἃ ἀκηκοας.   3. οἱ δουλοι του ἀρχοντος πεποιηκασιν το ἐργον. 4. ὁ δε ἀπεκρινατο, Ὃ γεγραφα, γεγραφα.   5. ὁτι δε γεγονα βασιλευς περιπατησω ἐν ταις ὁδοις των πατερων μου.   6. οἱ πτωχοι και οἱ τυφλοι βεβληνται εἰς φυλακην.   7. ὦ Κυριε, εἰς σε πεπιστευκαμεν.   8. λογιζομαι γαρ μηδεν ἀξιον αὐτον θανατου πεπραχεναι.   9. ὁ δε Υἱος του ἀνθρωπου ὑπαγει καθως γεγραπται περι αὐτου.   10. ἀπηγγελκαμεν γαρ την δευτεραν παρουσιαν αὐτου.   11. ὁ βασιλευς της δοξης ἠρται.   12. βεβληκεν δε τα βιβλια εἰς τον ποταμον.   13. και ἐγνωκα τας πονηρας ὁδους ὑμων.

---

[1] The passive of συναγω is often best translated by an active verb.
[2] The rule that the indicative is negatived by οὐ and the other moods by μη has exceptions. εἰ μη is often found with the indicative.

14. τη δε τριτη ἡμερᾳ ὁ Θεος ἠγειρεν τον Ἰησουν.   15. την πιστιν
τετηρηκα.   16. οἰδαμεν ὁτι ἀληθης εἶ.   17. αὐτος γαρ ἠδει το
σημειον ὃ ἐμελλεν ποιησαι.   18. ὁ κοσμος ὁλος ἐν τῳ πονηρῳ
κειται.   19. ὁ δε Πετρος ἐκαθητο ἐξω.   20. ἠκουσαν αὐτον
πεποιηκεναι τουτο το τερας.

35A

1. And Jesus was led by the Spirit into the mountains to be tempted by
the devil.   2. And the women were encouraged by their husbands.
3. Therefore my name shall be proclaimed among all the Gentiles.
4. For by grace were we saved through faith.   5. The dead will be
raised on the day of judgement by the voice of the angel.   6. And
when the demon was cast out the crowd wondered, and many said,
These wonders were not done in the days of our fathers.   7. After
these things he appeared to (was seen by) all the apostles.   8. He
commanded the man to be carried through the city.   9. On that day
all the people will be called holy to the Lord.   10. And the chief
priest was hidden in the mountains many years.   11. For I will make
my words to be heard by their ears.   12. None of the messengers
will be heard.   13. All the fish were thrown into the water.
14. These things were said through the mouth of David.   15. Let
one of the priests be sent to be persuaded by the king.   16. When the
good seed bore fruit the tares appeared also.   17. Teacher, you will
be loved by all the nation.   18. The bodies of the saints were sown
in dishonour, but they will be raised in glory.   19. Let them be
called foolish by the wise men of this age.   20. No temptation has
taken you.   21. For God has said this by the mouth of all the
prophets.   22. You will be led to kings and rulers because of my
name.   23. And darkness had already come (it had already become
dark) and Jesus had not yet come to them.   24. Do you know that
the Pharisees were scandalised?   25. Alas! They have had tribulation day and night.   26. For he has been persuaded by evil tongues
and has fallen into sin.   27. Because we have not been (are not)
judged by them, we have not judged (do not judge) them.   28. Let
these words be written, and let the people drink out of the scriptures.

35B

1. Παν το γενος τουτο ἐκληθη δικαιον. 2. πολλα των ῥηματων τουτων ἐγραφη ἐν βιβλιῳ ὑπο του ἀρχιερεως. 3. οἱ ἰχθυες ἐλημφθησαν ὑπο των παιδων τουτων. 4. ἐσπαρημεν ἐν θλιψει, ἐγερθησομεθα ἐν δυναμει. 5. το δαιμονιον ἐκβληθησεται και ὁ ὀχλος θαυμασει. 6. το καλον σπερμα ἠνεχθη εἰς τα ἐξ σκευη. 7. ἀπεσταλην δε ὑπο των διακονων του βασιλεως ζητειν σε. 8. γινωσκομεν (ἐγνωκαμεν, οἰδαμεν) ὁτι τουτο το εὐαγγελιον κηρυχθησεται πασιν τοις ἐθνεσιν και πολλοι ἀκουσουσιν. (The deponent middle is often used: ἀκουσονται.) 9. ἐν ἐκεινῃ τῃ ἡμερᾳ πολλα σωματα των ἁγιων ἠγερθη, και ἠλθεν εἰς την πολιν, και ἐφανη (ὠφθη) πολλοις. 10. θελομεν τα προβατα ἀχθηναι εἰς τα ὀρη. 11. σωθησῃ δε πιστει και ἐλπιδι. 12. παρηγγειλατε τους λιθους βληθηναι εἰς το ὑδωρ. 13. παντα ταυτα ποιηθησεται ἐν τῳ σκοτει. 14. ἠκουσατε ὁτι ἐρρηθη ὑπο των πατερων ἡμων ὁτι Οὐ ποιησεις εἰκονα. (This is a Hebrew idiom, familiar to us in the Authorised Version. The Future Indicative is used to express a command or prohibition.) 15. ἀσθενεις μεν ἐκληθημεν ὑπο πολλων, οἰδαμεν δε ὁτι αἱ συνειδησεις ἡμων ἀληθεις εἰσιν. 16. ἑωρακαμεν (ἑορακαμεν) και μεμαρτυρηκαμεν ὁτι οὑτος ἐστιν προφητης. 17. οἱ δε νεανιαι ἐστραφησαν ἀπο των ἁμαρτιων αὐτων ὁτι φοβος μεγας εἰληφει αὐτους. 18. ὁ οὐν Κυριος κακα εἰρηκεν περι σου. 19. ἐγω μεν εὑρηκα ὑμιν τους λογους της βασιλειας, ὑμεις δε οὐ πεπιστευκατε μοι. 20. παρηγγειλαν δε την θυσιαν ἀχθηναι προς τον ναον. 21. ὠ οἰκε Ἰσραηλ, μη κριθητι ὑπο των ἀπιστων. 22. οὐκ εἰρηται ἐν τῳ νομῳ ὁτι Οὐδεν σωθησεται; 23. ὑμας σεσωκεν· ἡμεις ὁμοιως σεσωσμεθα. 24. και πεπωκαμεν το ποτηριον της χαρας ὁ ἀπεσταλκεν ὁ Θεος. 25. ἰδου, κεκληκα αὐτον. 26. γυναι, σπαρηθι ἐν ὀργῃ, ἀλλ᾽ ἐγερθητι ἐν ἀγαπῃ. 27. ἐνηνοχα δε μερος της τιμης εἰς το της χηρας μνημειον.

36A

1. And as he was going along by the Sea of Galilee he saw Simon. 2. And he went preaching in their synagogues and casting out demons. 3. How hard it will be for those who have riches to enter the kingdom of God. 4. And those that ate the loaves were five thousand men.

5. And those who were scattered abroad went about preaching the word.   6. Jesus says to him, Because you have seen me, have you believed? Blessed are they that have not seen, and yet have believed. 7. And hearing these words Ananias fell down and died, and great fear came upon all who heard.   8. And the unclean spirit cried with a loud voice and came out of him.   9. And he was in the desert forty days and forty nights being tempted by Satan.   10. Therefore hear the parable of the sower.   11. And there appeared to them Moses and Elijah talking with him.   12. There comes to him Mary who was called Magdalene from whom seven demons had gone out.   13. To the church of God which is in Corinth.   14. Beginning from the baptism of John until this day.   15. This Jesus who was taken up from you to heaven will come again.   16. And do not be afraid of those who kill the body but are not able to kill the soul; fear rather him who is able to destroy both soul and body in hell.   17. And they went and reported to the chief priests all that had happened.   18. And ought not this woman, (being) a daughter of Abraham whom Satan bound for eighteen years, to be loosed on the sabbath day?   19. But Cornelius, having called together his relations, greeted him.   20. But he, knowing their hypocrisy, said to them, Why do you tempt me? 21. But the woman, knowing what had happened to her, came and fell down before him.   22. Fear him who, after he has killed, has power to cast into hell.

36B

1. Οἱ δε κηρυξαντες τον λογον απεσταλησαν ὑπο του Πνευματος. 2. και ἐλθοντες προς την θαλασσαν της Γαλιλαιας οἱ μαθηται ἐδιδαξαν πολλους.   3. μακαριοι οἱ ἀκουοντες και οἱ πιστευοντες τοις λογοις του βιβλιου τουτου.   4. πολλοι οὖν των τελωνων ἐβαπτισθησαν μετανοουντες ἀπο των ἁμαρτιων αὐτων.   5. ὁ δε ἀποκριθεις εἶπεν, Οὐκ εἰσελευσεσθε εἰς την βασιλειαν των οὐρανων. 6. ὁ σπειρων σπειρει τα σπερματα.   7. ἐξελθων δε εἶδεν μεγαν σταυρον.   8. ἐφοβουμεθα δε μη πιστευοντες ὅτι το ἐλεος αὐτου ἀληθες ἐστιν.   9. και παντες οἱ ἀκουσαντες ἐτηρησαν την ἐπαγγελιαν ἐν ταις καρδιαις αὐτων.   10. οὗτος γαρ ἐστιν ὁ πεμφθεις ὑπο του βασιλεως.   11. διδασκοντες δε τον λαον ἐμενον ἐν τῳ ἱερῳ. 12. και ἐξελθων ἐκ της πολεως ἀπηλθεν εἰς ἑτερον (ἀλλον) τοπον.

13. ὁ δὲ προφήτης ἔκραξεν λεγων, Ἰδου ὁ ἐρχομενος ὀπισω μου·
αὐτου ἀκουσετε.   14. ὁ οὖν ἀρχων ἀκουσας τουτο ἐφοβειτο και
παντες οἱ μετ᾽ αὐτου ὀντες.   15. ὁ δὲ ἀνηρ αὐτης δικαιος ὢν
ἠθελεν ἀπολυσαι αὐτην.   16. και ἐλθοντες εἰς την πολιν οἱ
φυλασσοντες αὐτην ἐξεβαλον αὐτους.   17. περιπατων δὲ δια των
ἀγρων εἰδον φως μεγα ἐκ του οὐρανου, και ἠκουσα φωνην λαλουσαν
μοι.   18. ὁ γραμματευς ἐμεινεν ἐν τῳ ὀρει τεσσαρακοντα ἡμερας
και τεσσαρακοντα νυκτας γραφων πασας τας ἐντολας του νομου.
19. ὁ μη ὢν μετ᾽ ἐμου κατ᾽ ἐμου ἐστιν.   20. ἐφοβειτο γαρ τον
Ἰωανην, εἰδως αὐτον ἀνδρα δικαιον.

37 A

1. And while Peter was still speaking these words the Holy Spirit fell
upon all that heard the word.   2. And since Lydda was near to
Joppa the disciples, hearing that Peter was there, sent two men to him.
3. This is the person who hears the word, and at once accepts it with
joy.   4. But you will receive power today, when the Holy Spirit has
come upon you.   5. Then they will see the Son of Man coming on
the clouds of heaven.   6. And he went away always proclaiming
what great things Jesus had done for him.   7. Jesus immediately saw
the Spirit of God coming down like a dove upon him.   8. And they
wondered at his answer and said nothing further.   9. Then there
came to him a certain woman asking something of him, and he said to
her, What do you now wish?   10. And all the multitude of the
people was praying outside.   11. And the whole city was already
gathered together at the door.   12. The Jerusalem that is now will
be trodden down again by the Gentiles.   13. For this thing has not
been done in a corner.   14. And the disciples of John were fasting.
15. For he was teaching them as one having authority, and not as their
scribes.   16. Behold now, nothing worthy of death has been done by
him.   17. And when day came he went out and went to a desert
place.   18. Go away to your home to your people and report to them
how much the Lord has done for you.   19. Now is the judgement of
this world.   20. For where your treasure is, there too will your heart
always be.   21. By what power or by what name did you do this?

22. How did you come in here without a wedding garment? 23. Where is your faith? 24. And when it had become late the boat was in the middle of the sea and he was alone on the land. (The feminine ὀψίας is used, ὥρας being understood.) 25. But he went out and began to proclaim these things again, with the result that Jesus was no longer able to enter the city openly. 26. You have kept the good wine till now. 27. But I say to you, Elijah has already come. 28. Then at once he said to the first, Work in the vineyard today. 29. And with many such parables he used to speak the word to them. 30. And a great multitude, hearing what great things he was doing, came to him no more. (*Note here the 'Construction according to Sense' (Lesson 32, n.1). This construction could be used in 37B9.*) 31. But now in Christ Jesus you have become near in the blood of Christ. 32. One thing I know that although I used to be blind now I see. 33. And when tribulation comes because of the word they at once stumble. 34. For as many of you as were baptised into Christ, put on Christ.

37B

1. Εἰσελθόντων δε των μαθητων εἰς το πλοιον ἀπεστειλεν ὁ Ἰησους τα πληθη εἰς τα ὀρη. 2. και (ἀνθρωπος) τις ἐλθων προς αὐτον εἰπεν, Τί ποιεις ὡδε; 3. τίνα δυναμιν λημψομεθα ἐλθοντος του Ἁγιου Πνευματος ἐφ' ἡμας; 4. της ἡμερας ἐγγισασης ὁ Υἱος του ἀνθρωπου ἐλευσεται μετα των νεφελων του οὐρανου. 5. ὁ δε Πετρος ἠλθεν προς αὐτον περιπατων ἐπι το ὑδωρ (or του ὑδατος or τῳ ὑδατι). 6. ἀπελθοντων δε των ἀγγελων οἱ μαθηται κατ' ἰδιαν ἐλαλησαν τῳ Ἰησου. 7. πεμψαντος δε αὐτου τον ἰδιον υἱον προς αὐτους, οὐκ ἠθελον δεχεσθαι αὐτον. 8. κρατουντος δε αὐτου την χειρα μου ἐδεξαμην δυναμιν περιπατειν. 9. ἐγγιζοντων δε αὐτων τῃ πολει ὁλον το πληθος ἐχαιρεν λεγον, Μακαριος (or, Perfect Participle Passive ηὐ- or εὐλογημενος) (ἐστιν) ὁ ἐρχομενος ἐν ὀνοματι του Κυριου. 10. και νυν δοξασον με, Πατερ. 11. πως δυνασθε ἀγαθα ἐτι λαλειν πονηροι ὀντες; 12. ἐν ποιᾳ ἐξουσιᾳ ταυτα ἐτι ποιεις; 13. ἡ θλιψις ἡ μεγαλη ἐγγυς ἐστιν. 14. λεγουσιν αὐτῳ, Που Κυριε; ἐρουμεν δε αὐτῳ, Πως Κυριε; 15. ὡδε ἐν Ἱεροσολυμοις ἐστιν ὁ τοπος ὁπου προσκυνειν δει. 16. πως

οὖν βλεπει ἀρτι;   17. ὁ μη πιστευων ἠδη κεκριται.   18. τίς δε
ἐστιν οὑτος περι οὑ ἀκουω τοιαυτα;   19. οἱ ἑκατονταρχαι ἠσαν
ἐσθιοντες και πινοντες.   20. τουτο πεπραγμενον ἐστιν ἐνωπιον
πολλων μαρτυρων.   21. ὡδε ἐσῃ περιπατων παντοτε ἐν τῃ ὁδῳ
της δικαιοσυνης.   22. τοτε πας ὁ ὀχλος ἠν συνηγμενος προς την
θαλασσαν.

38A

1. You set aside the commandment of God in order that you may keep your tradition.   2. Let us go into the other villages, in order that I may preach there also.   3. Whoever receives one of such children in my name, receives me; and whoever receives me, receives not me, but him who sent me.   4. And they shut their eyes, lest they should see with their eyes.   5. Whatever you bind on earth will be bound in heaven. (*Note here the Periphrastic Future Perfect.*)   6. Sirs, what must I do to be saved?   7. You will hear according to all that he says to you.   8. Shall we say then, Let us do evil that good may come?   9. For you have the poor always, and whenever you wish you can do them good.   10. Flee to Egypt and remain there until I tell you.   11. And he appointed twelve to be with him.   12. Wherever this gospel is preached in the whole world, it shall also be told what this woman has done.   13. Whoever does not receive the kingdom of God as a child shall on no account enter it.   14. When (i.e. As long as) I am in the world, I am the light of the world.   15. But, so that we may not give them offence, go to the sea and cast a hook.   16. Bring me word, that I too may come and worship him.   17. For they feared the people lest they might be stoned (i.e. they were afraid of being stoned by the people).   18. For it is better for you that one of your members should perish and not that your whole body should be cast into hell.   19. But pray that your flight may not be on a Sabbath. 20. And certain of those who are here shall not taste of death until they see the Son of Man.   21. Let us put on the weapons of light. 22. I write (wrote) these things to you that you may (might) know that you have eternal life.   23. And everything you ask in prayer you will receive, if you have faith.

38B

1. Οἱ γαρ Φαρισαιοι οὐκ ἐτηρουν τὴν ἐντολὴν του Θεου ἱνα τὴν ἰδιαν παραδοσιν τηρωσιν.   2. ὁ ἂν λεγω ὑμιν κατ' ἰδιαν κηρυσσετε παντι τῳ λαῳ.   3. τί οὖν ποιησωμεν; μενωμεν ἐν ἁμαρτιᾳ ἱνα περισσευῃ ἡ χαρις;   4. ὅταν ἰδητε τα ἐθνη ἐν τῳ ἁγιῳ τοπῳ, το τελος του αἰωνος ἐγγιζει.   5. ὅπου ἂν το εὐαγγελιον κηρυχθῃ οἱ πιστευοντες σωθησονται.   6. πεμψον τα τεκνα εἰς τὴν ἐρημον ἱνα μη ἀποκτεινωσιν αὐτα οἱ ἱερεις.   7. φαγωμεν και πιωμεν, δει γαρ ἡμας ὑπαγειν. (The Aorist might seem more appropriate here, but ὑπαγω is only found in the Present and Imperfect in the New Testament, see 25 A 15 n.)   8. ὁ Θεος πολλους προφητας ἀπεστειλεν διδασκειν (ἱνα διδασκωσιν) τον λαον τουτον.   9. πορευωμεθα εἰς ἀλλας πολεις παρακαλειν (ἱνα παρακαλωμεν) τα πληθη.   10. ὅταν θελωμεν δυναμεθα ἐλεειν τους πτωχους.   11. μεινον (μενε) ἐν τῃ οἰκιᾳ ἑως (or add ἂν, οὐ or ὁτου) καλεσω σε.   12. ἠραμεν παντα τα δενδρα ἱνα μη ἡμων οἱ ἐχθροι φαγωσιν τον καρπον.   13. οὐ πιομαι οἰνον ὁπως μη σκανδαλισω τον ἀδελφον μου.   14. φυλασσε τα προβατα ἑως ἂν εὑρω το μικρον μου.   15. ὃς ἂν θελῃ μειζων ἐν ὑμιν εἰναι ποιησατω ἑαυτον ὡς παιδιον.   16. ἐνεγκε τα ἱματια εἰς ἐμε ἱνα ἐνεχθῃ εἰς τας χηρας.   17. και παρεκαλει αὐτον ἱνα μετ' αὐτου ᾖ.   18. προσευχεσθε ἱνα μη ἐλθητε εἰς πειρασμον.

39A

1. For if you do good to those that do good to you, what reward do you have?   2. But Paul called out with a loud voice, saying, Do yourself no harm, for we are all here.   3. Unless your righteousness exceeds that of the scribes and Pharisees, you will on no account enter the kingdom of heaven.   4. If you wish to enter into life, keep the commandments.   5. If I have spoken evil, bear witness of the evil. 6. If I were still pleasing men, I should not be the slave of Christ. 7. If anyone is willing to do his will, he will know about the teaching. 8. Do not say (continue to say, make a practice of saying), What are we to eat? Or, What are we to drink?   9. If my kingdom were of this world, my servants would fight.   10. If we had been in the days of

our fathers, we should not have been sharers in the blood of the prophets.
11. And all debated in their hearts about John, whether he were the
Christt.   12. If the head of the house had known at which watch the
thief would come, he would have watched.   13. If this plan is[1] of
men, it will fail; but if it is of God, you will not be able to overthrow it.
14. Your money perish with you.   15. For if you had known what
this means, I desire mercy and not sacrifice, you would not have con-
demned the innocent.   16. But if we say, From men, all the people
will stone us, for they believe John to be a prophet.   17. Do not
(begin to) think that I came to destroy the law or the prophets.   18. Behold the bondmaid of the Lord; may it happen to me according to your
word.   19. Woe to you, Chorazin! Woe to you, Bethsaida! Because
if the mighty works that have been done in you had been done in Tyre
and Sidon, they would have repented long ago in sackcloth and ashes.
20. What shall we say then? Shall we remain in sin so that grace may
abound? God forbid.   21. Lord, if you had been here, my brother
would not have died.   22. If I were his son, he would be my father.
23. If some were unfaithful, will their faithlessness nullify the faithful-
ness of God? Heaven forbid. Let God be true, though every man be
false.   24. For all things are yours, whether Paul or Apollos or
Cephas, whether the world or life or death, all are yours, and you are
Christ's and Christ is God's.

39B

1. Κυριε, ἐαν θελῃς δυνασαι με καθαρισαι.   2. μη ἀγαγῃς τα
ἐθνη εἰς το ἱερον.   3. μη ζητωμεν τα του αἰωνος τουτου.   4. ὁ
οὖν νομος (ἐστιν) κατα των ἐπαγγελιων του Θεου; μη γενοιτο.
5. εἰ συ ἦς (ἦσθα) ἡ μητηρ μου, αὐτος ἦν ὁ ἀδελφος μου.   6. εἰ συ
ἦσθα (ἦς) ἡ μητηρ μου, αὐτος ἀν ἦν ὁ ἀδελφος μου.   7. εἰ με
ᾐδειτε, και τον πατερα μου ἀν ᾐδειτε.   8. μη δεχεσθε τους ἐχθρους
του εὐαγγελιου.   9. γενοιτο ἡμιν κατα το θελημα σου.   10. εἰ
τυφλοι ἦτε οὐκ ἀν εἰχετε ἁμαρτιαν.   11. εἰ νεκροι οὐκ ἐγειρονται,

---

[1] Acts 5. 38 f. A present condition expressed by ἐαν with subjunctive is un-
usual. An element of uncertainty may be suggested: 'If (as one may suppose)
this plan be...but if (as these persons claim) it really is.' Or there may be a
future element: 'If this plan turn out to be.'

οὐδε Χριστος ἐγηγερται.   12. μηκετι ἁμαρτανε.   13. μη ἐνεγ-
κης οἰνον προς τους δουλους.   14. ἐαν ὁ ἐχθρος ἐγγιση, ἀποστελω
κατ᾽ αὐτου τους στρατιωτας.   15. μη κρινετε, ἱνα μη (ὁπως μη,
μη) κριθητε.

40 A

1. And he asked of them where Christ was to be born.   2. He is not a
God of the dead, but of the living, for all live to him.   3. This word
is not being made known to us.   4. They spoke of his departure
which he was about to fulfil in Jerusalem.   5. Simon (son of) John,
do you love me more than these?   6. Then they crucified with him
two robbers.   7. And having heard a crowd passing through he
asked what this meant.   8. Why do you ask me about the good?
9. Jesus says to him, Go. Your son lives.   10. I will on no account
eat it until it is fulfilled in the kingdom of God.   11. If you love me,
you will keep my commandments.   12. For if you love those who
love you, what reward do you have?   13. So that that which was
spoken through the prophets might be fulfilled.   14. And his disciples
asked him what this parable meant.   15. If you loved me, you would
have rejoiced that I am going to the Father.   16. If God was your
Father, you would love me.   17. You are led astray (mistaken), not
knowing the scriptures nor the power of God.   18. The sons of this
age are begotten (born) and beget.   19. See that you say nothing to
anyone.   20. He who does not honour the Son does not honour the
Father.   21. But he warned them to tell no one.   22. We boast
(let us boast) in hope of the glory of God.   23. Everyone who
believes is being justified.   24. See (to it); let no one know.   25. And
calling one of the servants he asked what these things might be.

40 B

1. Οἱ μαθηται ἐφανερουν ταυτα ἁ ἠκουσαν.   2. μη σταυρουτε
δουλους.   3. μελλουσιν ζην ἐν τη πολει ἡμων;   4. θελετε ἀρα
ἀγαπαν Κυριον τον Θεον ὑμων;   5. νυν πληρουται ὁ λογος του
προφητου.   6. ὁ δε Θεος δικαιοι τους υἱους των ἀνθρωπων πιστει
και οὐκ ἐργοις.   7. ὁ υἱος σου ζη.   8. ἐφανερωσα γαρ το ὀνομα

σου τουτῳ τῳ λαῳ, και φανερωσω αυτο τοις τεκνοις αυτων.   9. ἐ-
θεωρουν το ἱερον πεπληρωμενον τῃ δοξῃ του Κυριου.   10. ὠ Πατερ,
φανερωσον την δυναμιν σου ἡμιν ἱνα δοξασθῃ το ὀνομα σου.   11. ἐαν
ποιητε ταυτα ἀγαπηθησεσθε ὑπο του πατρος μου.   12. ἐαν
ἀγαπωμεν αὐτον τηρησομεν τας ἐντολας αὐτου.   13. και ἠλθον
προς τον ἱερεα ἱνα ἐρωτησωσιν αὐτον περι της συνειδησεως αὐτων.
14. οὐ μη φανερωσω ἐμαυτον τῳ γενει τουτῳ.   15. και εἰς των
γραμματεων, εἰδως ὁτι καλως ἀπεκριθη αὐτοις, ἐπηρωτησεν αὐτον.
16. πεπληρωται ὁ καιρος.   17. ἡμεις δε κηρυσσομεν Χριστον
ἐσταυρωμενον.   18. ὁ πλουσιος ὁρᾳ Ἀβρααμ.   19. τιμα την
μητερα σου.   20. οἱ δε μαθηται ἐπετιμων αὐτοις.   21. μηδεις
πλανατω (πλανησατω) ὑμας.   22. ὁ καυχωμενος ἐν Κυριῳ καυ-
χασθω.   23. τοτε ὁ τυφλος ἠρωτησεν τί ἀν εἰη τουτο.

41 A

1. Men do not light a lamp and put it outside the door.   2. And
Joseph took the body and placed it in his new tomb.   3. Does the
lamp come so that it may be put outside?   4. And he blesses the
children, laying his hands upon them.   5. The good shepherd lays
down his life for the sheep.   6. They have taken the Lord out of the
tomb, and we do not know where they nave laid him.   7. It is not
yours to know times or seasons which the Father has put within his own
authority.   8. And they sought to bring him in and lay him before
him.   9. And he knelt down and prayed.   10. I will lay down my
life for your sake.   11. Pray always until I make your enemies a
footstool for your feet.   12. This is the throne that was placed in the
temple.   13. I shall come down to place my hands upon her, and
she will live.   14. The nets were placed beside the boat.   15. Do
not lay (make a practice of laying) hands on anyone.   16. They saw
where he was laid.   17. A new tomb in which no one had yet been
placed.   18. Why is it that you have contrived (R.S.V.) this deed in
your heart?   19. And they put Peter in prison.   20. Every Sunday
let each of you put (something) aside.   21. The sword is being placed
in the hand of the king.

41 B

1. Δει ἡμας τιθεναι τον νομον της ἀγαπης ἐν ταις καρδιαις ἡμων καθ' ἡμεραν.   2. τιθετε ἐκει την χαραν ὁμοιως.   3. που τεθεικατε αὐτον;   4. πως θωμεν την θυγατερα ἡμων παρα τους ποδας αὐτου;   5. ἐθεντο τα βιβλια αὐτων ἐν τῃ συναγωγῃ.   6. και ἡμεις θησομεν αὐτα ἐκει.   7. τεθεικας με ἐν ἀγαθῃ γῃ.   8. θετε τας ψυχας ὑμων ὑπερ των ἀδελφων.   9. μη θῃς ταυτην την γραφην ἐπι τον σταυρον (or genitive or dative).   10. θετε το σωμα ἐν τῳ μνημειῳ.   11. οἱ ἀποστολοι κατηυλογησαν ἡμας ἐπιτιθεντες τας χειρας ἐφ' ἡμας.   12. ὁ δε ἀσθενης εἰσηνεχθη και ἐτεθη ἐνωπιον αὐτου.   13. ἐλθων ἐπιθες την χειρα σου ἐπ' αὐτην.

42 A

1. And I give you authority to cast out unclean spirits.   2. For God gives the Holy Spirit to them that ask him.   3. Who is it that gave you this authority?   4. I wish you to give me the head of John.   5. And why did you not give my money to the poor?   6. To you it is given to know the mysteries of the kingdom.   7. If you owe anything, pay me!   8. But he would not, but went away and cast him into prison until he should pay the debt.   9. Is it lawful to give taxes to Caesar or not? Shall we give, or shall we not give?   10. All authority in heaven and on earth was given to me.   11. The Father loves the Son and has given all things into his hand.   12. It is more blessed to give than to get.   13. What is the wisdom which is given to this man?   14. Tell me if you sold the land.   15. I will give you all these things, if you will fall down and worship me.   16. And when they lead you away and hand you over, do not be anxious beforehand what to say, but say whatever is given you in that hour.   17. For you know (how) to give good gifts to your children.   18. But the chief priests had given orders.

42 B

1. Παντοτε ἀποδιδου παντα ἁ ἐχεις.   2. σημερον δος τοις πτωχοις.   3. θελομεν δουναι αὐτο τοις ἀρχιερευσιν.   4. ἐδοθη μοι ὑπο του πατρος μου.   5. μη διδου ἀγαθα τοις πονηροις.   6. περιεπατουν δε διδοντες ἱματια τοις λεπροις.   7. οὐ μη δω (or, δωσω) το σον τῳ

Κυριῳ.   8. ἐδωκας δε μοι ὑδωρ.   9. τηρησωμεν τας ἐντολας
τας ἡμιν διδομενας.   10. ὁ διδους ἀρτον τοις ἀσθενεσιν ἑξει τον
μισθον αὐτου.   11. ὁ βασιλευς ἡμιν δεδωκεν ταυτην την πολιν · μη
παραδωμεν αὐτην τοις ἐχθροις αὐτου.   12. ἡ ἀφεσις διδοται ἡμιν.

43 A

1. Then the devil takes him to the holy city and he set him on the pinnacle of the temple.   2. And while they were saying these things he himself stood in the midst of them.   3. They saw the man who had been healed standing with them.   4. Man, who appointed me a judge over you?   5. Now God commands men that they should all everywhere repent, because he has fixed a day in which he is about to judge the world in righteousness.   6. The Pharisee having taken his stand prayed thus to himself.   7. But the publican standing at a distance was not willing even to lift his eyes to heaven.   8. But Jesus stood before the governor.   9. And having knelt down he cried out with a loud voice, Lord, do not put this sin to their account.   10. After this Judas the Galilean rose up in the days of the enrolment.   11. If they do not hear Moses and the prophets, they will not be persuaded even if someone rises from the dead.   12. And I shall raise him up at the last day.   13. His mother and his brothers were standing outside desiring to speak to him.   14. The hypocrites love to pray standing in the synagogues.   15. And giving her his hand he raised her up.   16. And he stood over her and rebuked the fever.   17. One day the chief priests came up and said.   18. But Jesus taking a child placed it by himself.   19. Go and take your stand in the temple and speak to the people all the words of this life.   20. Tell the vision to no one until the Son of Man is raised from the dead.   21. To whom also he presented himself alive after he had suffered.   22. And coming up he touched the bier, and those who were carrying it stood still.   23. And they set up false witnesses who said, This man does not cease to speak words against the holy place.   24. And they brought them and set them in the council.   25. Put on the whole armour of God so that you may be able to stand.

45

43 B

1. Στησω σε ἐν σκοτει. 2. εἰσιν τινες των ὧδε ἑστωτων (ἑστη-
κοτων). 3. δει οὖν τον Παυλον στηναι ἐν τῳ συνεδριῳ. 4. οἱ
ἱερεις ἐστησαν ἐκει τον τελωνην. 5. ὁ δε Πετρος ἀναστας ἐκηρυξεν
τον λογον τῳ ὀχλῳ. 6. οὐκ ἐστιν ὧδε, ἀνεστη γαρ ἐκ νεκρων.
7. τίς σε κατεστησεν ἀρχοντα του λαου τουτου; 8. τοτε ἀνασταν-
τες ἀπηλθομεν ἐκ της πολεως. 9. ἐστησατε τον βασιλεα ἐν τῳ
ἁγιῳ τοπῳ. 10. πως στωμεν ἐν τῃ ἡμερᾳ της ὀργης αὐτου;
11. ἑστημεν ἐξω θελοντες ἰδειν τον ἀνδρα αὐτης. 12. μετα ταυτα
πολλοι πονηροι ἀνεστησαν. 13. ἐλπιζομεν στηναι ἐν ἐκεινῃ τῃ
ἡμερᾳ. 14. τοτε το Πνευμα του Κυριου κατεστησεν με φως τοις
πληθεσιν. 15. εἰ τις πιστευει εἰς ἐμε ἀναστησω αὐτον ἐν τῃ
ἐσχατῃ ἡμερᾳ. 16. ἡ δε μητηρ αὐτου ἐξω εἰστηκει.

44

1. Then the devil leaves him. 2. But he says, All sin and blasphemy
will be forgiven to men. 3. Let the children come to me and do not
(continue to) hinder them. 4. But Jesus cried out again and let his
spirit depart. 5. But everything is in parables lest they should turn
and it be forgiven them. 6. And you no longer allow him to do
anything for his father. 7. I tell you, her sins which are many are
forgiven. 8. Who is this who even forgives sins? 9. Behold
your house is forsaken. (*This is a Futuristic Present. Just as the Historic
Present is frequently used in both Greek and English (notably in St
Mark) to express a past event graphically, so a Futuristic Present can
be used to express a future event graphically.*) 10. Forgive if you
have anything against anybody. 11. They will not leave one stone
upon another in you. 12. If you forgive the sins of any, they are
forgiven them. 13. This is the person who hears the word and
understands it. 14. Hear me, all of you, and understand. 15. But
he said, Lord, save, we are perishing. 16. For Herod is about to
seek the child to destroy it. 17. But go rather to the lost sheep.
18. He who finds his life will lose it. 19. For all who take the sword
will perish by the sword. 20. Can a prophet perish outside Jeru-

salem?   21. For the word of the cross is folly to those who are perishing.   22. I will destroy the wisdom of the wise.   23. What am I saying then?   24. As certain say we say.   25. Permit it now, he says, for it is fitting for us in this way to fulfil all righteousness. Then he permits him.   26. Then the disciples understood that he spoke to them of John the Baptist.   27. Who can forgive sins but one, that is God?   28. And immediately they left the nets and followed him. 29. And forgive us our debts as we too have forgiven our debtors. 30. For if you forgive men their trespasses, your heavenly Father will also forgive you.   31. Then the devil shows him all the kingdoms of the world.   32. But to those that are without all is done in parables, that hearing they may hear and not understand.   33. But Jesus gave the bread to the disciples that they might give it to the crowds.   34. And wherever he entered they laid the sick in the market places.   35. And they put the money at the apostles' feet.   36. And he gave the loaves to the disciples to set before them.   37. How then shall his kingdom stand?   38. Give and it shall be given you.   39. And Jesus said, Rise. And he rose and stood.

Published by the Press Syndicate of the University of Cambridge
The Pitt Building, Trumpington Street, Cambridge CB2 IRP
40 West 20th Street, New York, NY 10011-4211, USA
10 Stamford Road, Oakleigh, Melbourne 3166, Australia

Library of Congress catalogue card number: 65-14858

ISBN 0 521 06769 3

First published 1965
Reprinted 1966 1970 1971 1973 1975 1977 1978
1980 1982 1983 1986 1988 1991

Printed in Great Britain at the
University Press, Cambridge